Your Brain Has a
Bent—(Not a Dent!)

Your Brain Has a
Bent—(Not a Dent!)

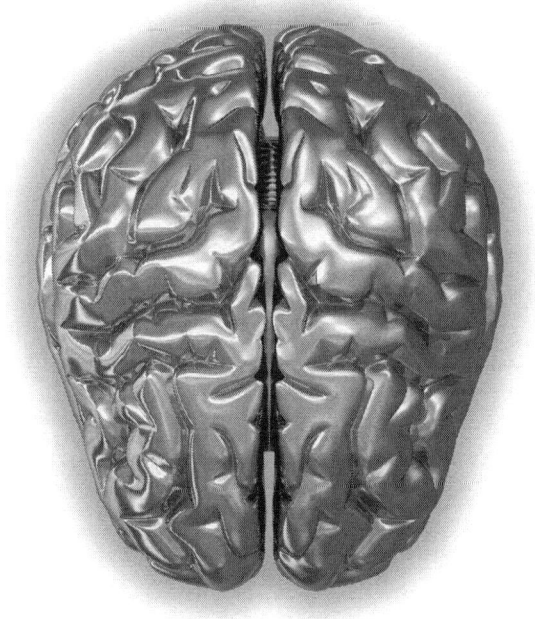

Arlene R. Taylor, PhD
W. Eugene Brewer, EdD

Success Resources International
Napa, California

P O Box 2554, Napa, CA 94558-9255 USA

ISBN # 1-887307-75-3

Special thanks to Michelle Nash.
Thanks to proof readers, including Candi Brewer.

Cover design by David Eastman:
        www.EastmanCreations.com

Contains some material previously included in the book *MindWaves*.

Scripture taken from the Holy Bible, New International version. Copyright © 1973, 1978, 1984 by International Bible Society. Used by permission of Zondervan Publishing House.

Quotes from Metaphors Dictionary by Elyse. Sommer and Dottie Weiss. Visible Ink Press, 1996. Reprinted by permission of Visible Ink Press.

About This Book

The authors simplify and clarify the essence of the power we have within ourselves. The choreography of the writing moves the reader from the right-brain to the left-brain . . . It is a satisfying dance of words.

> —Thea S. Spatz, EdD, CHES, Professor,
> University of Arkansas at Little Rock

A refreshing look at how people think and learn. Real people stories . . . a must read for all who teach, and all who journey with exhilaration into their own continuing growth.

> —Bernice McCarthy PhD
> President, About Learning Inc

Delightful and enjoyable . . . written with humor and in a light-hearted style . . . It's about time we had a book like this around.

> —Sam Carter Gilliam MA
> Performing Artist/Teacher

This treasure trove is one of the most innovative, fascinating books yet to appear.

> —Clif St. Germain PhD
> The Center for Academic Excellence

This [book] helps simplify the many complexities of your amazing brain.

> —Roy Drusky, Grand Ole Opry Star

Publisher's Reminder

This book is not a biological, medical, or psychological text. The information and resources offered are for general educational and informational purposes only and do not present an in-depth treatment of specific research findings or topics. They are not intended to take the place of professional counseling, medical or psychological care, or recommendations from healthcare professionals.

Be sure to consult with your physician or healthcare professional before you make lifestyle changes or add physical exercising to your daily regimen.

The publisher, authors, and editors expressly disclaim all responsibility and any liability (direct or indirect) for adverse effects from the use or misuse of concepts presented herein.

If you find errors/typos in this book, please know that they are there for a purpose. The authors wanted to write something for everyone, and some "brains" really enjoy looking for mistakes.

Contents

Dedication

Your Brain Has a Bent—(Not a Dent) is dedicated to the memory of Ann Woods Bell, whose interest in the human brain and pursuit of knowledge about it was life-long.

It is also dedicated to the many who have expressed an interest in obtaining an easy-reading introduction to brain-function information. We hope this material makes a positive difference in your life as it has in ours.

Researching the information and writing this book has undoubtedly helped to stimulate our brains and further our interest in uncovering helpful brain-function secrets, explanations, and practical applications.

Thank you!

Point To Ponder

The chief function of your body is to carry your brain around.

—Thomas Alva Edison

Foreword

If it is to be—it is up to me.

Old Proverb

I*f you can read this, thank a teacher,* says the bumper sticker. If you read this book, your brain will thank you. Why? Most brains are involved in reading, and many other things, without fulfillment, enjoyment, or even practical gain. We recite the ABCs and other required educational tasks, yet many still lack the ability to cash in—or even crash in—on doing well, living well, or being well.

Before you assume this is just another health book, or just another "brain" book, think again. Within its covers, *Your Brain Has a Bent (Not a Dent)* offers clear illustrations and factual morsels that could mean the difference between a life well-lived and just marking time in this world, and between being well and simply being.

Thousands of electrochemical events occur within your mind every nanosecond. These events, past and present, are a virtual textbook of memories and moments that are keys to unlocking the wonders and power in your mind.

I am a physician who travels the world in search of discoveries that can bring the rewards of healing and health, which begins and ends in your brain. Why have I linked the content of *Your Brain Has a Bent (Not a Dent)* with health? The World Health Organization's definition of health (which has not been amended since 1948, an indication of its worldwide acceptance) is the universal standard to measure health. It says:

Health is a state of complete physical, mental, and social well-being and not merely the absence of disease or infirmity.

This book is more than a collection of stories about surfing brains or how nature and nurture impact one's brain. It is also a workbook you can use to achieve a state of health most people don't possess. It will help you unlock the passion in your relationships, discover (or recover) the purpose in life that was imprinted upon your DNA at conception, and foster the unadulterated whole-brain intelligence of your children, loves, and co-workers.

 We live in an ever-interconnected world of relationships where one person does make a difference. The brain health of one soul can be more infectious than any Mad Cow virus. The inner soul desires, fuels, hopes, and dreams of a state of complete physical, mental, and social well being.

Each of us deserves more out of life and can have more, even the abundant life. It begins by personally connecting your brain to your hopes, or creating a new vision of desires. Living is more than the mundane day in and day out business of life. Seek the facts that are rooted in timeless truths. You will find them in this book.

But you cannot simply give assent to expert data. Active participation is crucial to change, progress, and to peak performance. If you desire more than a humdrum existence, the mind has the capacity for infinite possibilities.

*What are you willing to do to grasp
such a state of health and well being?*

The fact that you have opened *Your Brain Has a Bent (Not a Dent)* suggests that you possess an unquenchable longing to do more than read a book and thank a teacher. You are becoming conscious of the fact that you are a living textbook and must allow your brain to teach you what cannot be found in a book.

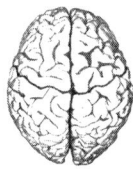 If your brain has *dents* from being sideswiped—or even intentionally broad-sided by unknowing (or well-meaning but unenlightened) parents, teachers, friends, colleagues, spouses, partners, or bosses—*Your Brain Has a Bent (Not a Dent)* is definitely a prescription for your healing and whole-brain health.

This book is for anybody who is curious about living the good life and making good things happen. I have read it, and thank Arlene and Gene for writing it.

Donna L. Willis, MD, MPH
Medical Contributor, ABC "The View"
Adjunct Faculty Johns Hopkins
University School of Medicine

Point To Ponder

The human brain operates both locally and holistically so it influences every organ in the body.

—Richard Restak, MD

Preface

The human brain is the most
complex mass of protoplasm on earth—
perhaps even in our galaxy.

Marian C. Diamond
Arnold B. Scheibel

I If you're like most people, even those who
have lived through the *decade of the* brain in
the '90s, *this complex mass of protoplasm* as
Diamond and Scheibel put it, is a bit of a
mystery. Nevertheless, your brain impacts your
entire body and your entire life.

If you are interested in doing everything you can
to understand and retain your brain function, and
committed to learn to use it by design to be more
successful in every area of life, then this book is
for you.

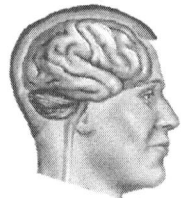 Studies have shown that the way
in which your brain functions
impacts not only who you are
innately, but also everything you
think, say, and do. The way you
relate to others, how successful
you are in your chosen career, and a host of other
facets are influenced by your brain's functions.

It has been said that whether you have little ability or great ability and excel in many things or only a few; whether you have one talent or ten talents is not of the greatest importance. Who you *are* and what you do with who you *are* is what counts.

Early in this 21st Century, many were talking about what they wanted. Media surveys showed that the majority of people wanted to be more successful. Of course, not everyone interprets success to mean the same thing. Some want better health, others improved relationships, others enhanced careers, still others increased financial security, while some want to hone their level of personal spirituality. Nevertheless, the overall theme was then, and is still,

I want to be more successful in life.

What would you do if you knew of a no-fail way to accomplish your success goal? Especially if it didn't require huge amounts of money or contracts with elusive gurus! Would you be interested? What if you knew that it would take time and effort; but how, when, and where would be up to you? Would you still be interested?

Bets are your answer would be a resounding *yes!* Truth is, a way to increase your likelihood of success *does exist:* it involves understanding and paying attention to your own brain.

Your Brain Has a Bent—(Not a Dent) is designed to help you get to know your own unique brain—that most mysterious, complex, and fascinating body organ; that most intricately organized and densely populated expanse of biological real estate in the world—and identify the advantages that it alone possesses.

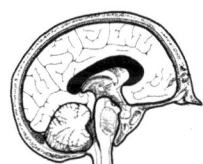 As Hammer and Copeland, authors of *Living With Our Genes: Why They Matter More than You Think,* put it:

Each of us is born into the world as someone; we spend the rest of our lives trying to find out who.

This is a personal journey. No one can do it for you, because your brain is not only unique, it is more interested in you than in anyone else on the planet.

As an old proverb states:

You are the only person who can be yourself; no one else has the qualifications for that job.

Your brain wants to collaborate with you and is anxious to do so. Use it by design for success.

Yours!

Point To Ponder

From the brain only arise our pleasures, joys, laughter, and jests, as well as our sorrows, pains, griefs, and tears...

—Hippocrates (460-377 BC)

Chapter One

Introduction: User's Guide for the Brain 101

The human mind, once exposed to a new idea, never returns to its original dimensions.

—Oliver Wendell Holmes

Have you noticed that every new car you've ever purchased—or microwave or telephone or outdoor grill—has come with an owner's manual? (Not that anyone actually reads it or can even find it when something goes wrong!)

The average person probably realizes that the most important *unit* in this incredible housing called the human body is the brain. Most people might even want to understand and effectively use their own brain. An owner's manual, a user's guide, is needed.

However, when folks go out to find a book on brains, they are usually dazzled—or is it daunted?—with five-pound-research books filled with charts and facts and figures, designed more for the scientist, the instructor, the philosopher, the physician, or the graduate student planning to write yet another textbook on the brain.

But where are the pictures? The stories? Where's the readability? Where's the chance that you could actually understand and apply the information?

This book is about *you*—really the only natural place to start. Because it's easier to understand and live with others when you first understand yourself. That is not a new concept!

Remember Socrates, the Greek philosopher in Athens (469 BC - 399 BC)? Millennia ago he became famous for arguing that one must 'Know Thyself' to be wise, and that the unexamined life is not worth living.

The "Who Am I?" Pyramid

This book also includes information related to the *"Who am I?" Pyramid*, a model designed to portray four key types of brain function. If you can identify how each relates to your brain, at least at some level, you can better manage your energy by design. The knowledge can help you practically apply the information to enhance your success both personally and professionally.

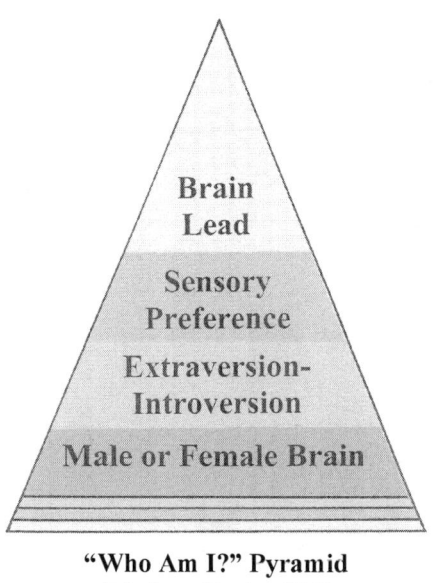

"Who Am I?" Pyramid
©Arlene Taylor PhD

1ˢᵗ Layer: Male or Female Brain

The first or foundational layer refers to the type of brain you possess in terms of:

- A systemizing brain associated with males

- An empathizing brain associated with females

- A balanced blend of both

- None of the above, estimated to be 5% of the general population

3

2nd Layer: Extraversion (Ambiversion) Introversion

The second layer of the *"Who Am I?" Pyramid* refers to the type of brain you possess in terms of an internal or external focus, and whether it functions best (most energy-efficiently) in a:

- Stimulating environment

- Non-stimulating environment

- Balanced environment

3rd Layer: Sensory Preference

The third layer of the *"Who Am I?" Pyramid* refers to the type of sensory stimuli that registers most quickly and intensely in your brain:

- Visual

  - Auditory

    - Kinesthetic

Your sensory preference impacts the way you process new information most easily, your comfort level in any given environmental situation, and the way in which you tend to interact with others and with your environment.

4th Layer: Brain Lead

The top layer refers to your brain's innate and unique energy advantage in one of the four natural divisions of the cerebrum or thinking layer. These can be referred to as:

- Prioritizing style

- Visualizing style

- Maintaining style

- Harmonizing style

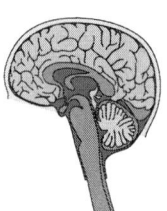

The top layer, your *brain lead/bent,* impacts the way you pay attention to and manage data. Figure that out and you can manage your brain's energy by design. You actually may have paid an enormous price—often ongoing—for the type of brain you received at birth.

If your brain's innate giftedness did not match societal expectations for your gender, you and your brain may have been undervalued by society. In fact, you may have thought your brain had a *dent* because of the mismatch.

Nevertheless, you can learn to thrive by identifying, honoring, and living your brain's preferences, its *bent.*

Research Studies

This book is backed up by (but not bogged down with) research. Moreover, it is relevant and simple—unlike that car manual which, if you *could* have found it, probably wasn't readable. It includes brain-function information.

The study of brain function is a branch of science that investigates the specific characteristic actions of the human brain. The research conclusions derive from many sources including:

- Traditional Disciplines (e.g., Biology, Physiology, Psychology, Neurology, Anatomy, Chemistry, Psychiatry)

- Structural and Functional Neuroimaging (e.g., PET, MRI, fMRI, MEG, CAT SPECT) that allow researchers to study brain structure and function while the individual is still alive.

A selected Bibliography is included should you desire to do additional reading.

The illustrations used are composites of real-life situations. Names and identifying details have been changed to protect confidentiality.

Owner's Manual

Think of this book as an owner's manual for the brain. It is designed for:

- The inquiring person

- The individual who has an inkling that learning about one's own brain and following specific principles could reduce symptoms of depression, burn-out, exhaustion, disease, midlife crisis, minor and major health issues, and relationship stressors

- Someone who wants to slow down the process of aging insofar as it is possible to do so, and maximize the use of his/her brain's unique giftedness

I've known folks who have had a car and are contented just knowing where the owner's manual is. *No need to sit around reading when you could be driving.* But I've never known a person who, after learning more about his or her own brain, said, "What a waste of time."

Like an oil change, such information will help your brain run more smoothly, like a tune-up you'll be purring along towards greater success, and, like a new wax job, you'll sense the glow. Enjoy the ride.

Point To Ponder

Some children end up paying an exorbitant price for having the kind of mind they were born with.

—Mel Levine in *A Mind at a Time*

Chapter Two

Your Brain's *Bent*

An ulcer, gentlemen, is an unkissed imagination taking its revenge for having been jilted. It is an unwritten poem, an undanced dance, an unpainted watercolor. It is a declaration . . . that a clear spring of joy has not been tapped.

J. Ciardi, addressing Canadian businessmen, 1952

No surprise—Grandpa had it right. But family members never would have dreamed how on target Gramps really was with casual comments such as, "Uncle Paul sure has a bent for puttin' things together." Or, "Little Margie does have a bent for writin' poetry." Or, "You've got a bent for cookin' sure as shootin'."

Long before brain research validated Grandpa's "bent" theory, he had a gut-sense of it. Of course, he assumed the "bent" was in Paul's dexterous fingers or Margie's way with words.

It's beyond amazing: your brain bent developed during gestation and arrived with your birth

9

package. Author and brain researcher Daniel Seigel puts it like this: "The left and right sides of the brain have distinct circuits that become predominant early in life, even in the embryo."

Recent research shows that a person's own special ability to do something easily and energy-efficiently—and enjoy it at the same time—resides in the brain. But that's not all. The brain also manages one's energy resources.

Hans Selye, sometimes referred to as the father of stress management, advocated paying attention to this "energy bank" and making withdrawals judiciously. Some activities require higher expenditures of energy, others lower, depending on the individual and his/her brin. Understanding and applying that single principle alone can likely add life to your years—and maybe even years to your life.

Jacob's Story

The day Jacob Smithey graduated from law school, he handed his diploma to his father. "There," he said, 'I'm finally the lawyer *you* wanted me to be. Now I'm leaving to become the writer *I've* always wanted to be."

Is something going on with Jacob—other than attitude and personal choice? Definitely. It's called *preference, innate giftedness, or calling*— something within the brain that wants a person to identify who he/she was really meant to be; something that wants to avoid expending more energy than is absolutely necessary. The very thing Grandpa called a "bent."

Bent—and Energy

Your brain is unique. Period. It has a *bent.* Oh yes, human brains are more alike than they are different, but each is unique, too. Washing and waxing a car is fun to one brain, absolute drudgery to the next. The same with cooking a gourmet meal, playing an instrument, or doing yard work. Even if you *can* balance your checkbook, you might find that activity (or even the very thought of it!) exhausting. Others are energized by working with numbers. Torture or treat—it's all about your brain's bent.

A huge difference can exist between learning to do something *well*—and doing it with *energy-efficiency.* The latter can exude a sense of play versus a sense of work. When these two concepts match (doing it well AND energy-efficiently), it becomes a win-win for your unique brain.

Typically, humans give up one thing for another. That's life. If you're going to do community service, reading your favorite author may have to wait until later. Since your body's basic medium of exchange is energy, the question becomes, *How are you using your brain's energy?*

Some believe that unless you match the majority of your life's activities with your brain's energy advantage, you could shorten your potential longevity by a decade or more. Did you pick up the impact of that? *Fail to use your brain energy-efficiently and you could die earlier.* That alone makes the conclusions from brain-function studies worth investigating.

Marci's Story

Marci works at a job she was educated to do: feature journalism. She has earned recognition for her stories, and a compilation of her best writing has been published in a journalism textbook. However, Marci is drained professionally. While *appearing* focused and energized, she drags herself to work every day. Privately, Marci admits, "I can't face another homeless family or desperate drop-out. I'd rather cover current events and do fact reporting."

*Choose a job you love and you'll
never work a day in your life.*
—Confucius

Preference Is an Advantage

Think of your brain's bent as a biochemical energy advantage. (Some have explained it as a reduced resistance to the transmission of information across the synaptic gap between neurons—in a specific section of your brain.)

When engaged in activities that match your brain's innate giftedness (energy advantage), you can generally expect noticeable changes in four main areas: competence, energy level, health, and overall outlook.

- Honoring your brain's bent usually helps you develop higher levels of competency. Of course, increased competence often contributes to increased success

- Your brain tends to expend less energy when engaged in an activity that matches its *bent*. This means your energy may last longer, since withdrawals from your energy bank are made in smaller increments

- The closer the match between your life's activities and your brain's bent, the more likely you are to be healthy, successful, happy, and achieve your longevity potential. When the reverse occurs and the majority of your activities are energy-exhausting), your risk rises for experiencing health problems, fatigue, discouragement, and you name it

- Because the brain and immune system are in constant communication, one way to strengthen your immune system is to keep your brain happy. In general, a happy brain makes for a happy body

Biochemical Advantage—In Real Life

If a teacher feels "called" to teach, that individual will likely achieve high levels of competence in that career, be energized in the classroom, have a lower absenteeism rate, and look forward to school starting each year.

A teacher who does not have that innate giftedness will be more likely to experience depression, fatigue, and burn-out. And even worse, may be a mediocre teacher.

Jeannie's Story

Jeannie had worked for eleven years as a supervisor in the billing department of a large insurance company. While competent to all external appearances, privately and internally she was experiencing burnout, suffering from depression, gaining weight. Most of the time she felt "plumb out of energy."

Several times Jeannie approached her boss about applying for another position as postings showed up on the "jobs available" board, but each time she allowed herself to be talked out of applying. "But you do it so *well*," her boss would say and Jeannie would drop the subject.

When her physician suggested medication, Jeannie decided to interview for Director of Volunteer Services. She was hired and within three months, even her former co-workers admitted that the position was a "great fit." Her depression gradually lifted even as her energy level increased. And her weight decreased.

John's Story

John, a college sophomore noted for his math skills, was selected by the math chair to be a peer tutor for struggling non-math majors. He acknowledged the honor, but didn't look forward to the job. "I don't like explaining math concepts," John said. "I'd much rather assist in the science lab." After two months in the math center, he quit—burned out, but concerned that he had disappointed his professors.

What these two individuals *wanted* to do, versus what they were *told* to do, demonstrates the concept of working within one's personal brain bent. While some folks might not understand that, technically most people are able to sense their brains nudging them towards where they belong—if they increase their awareness and pay attention to the messages their bodies are trying to give them.

According to Carl Gustav Jung, renowned Swiss Psychiatrist and founder of analytic psychology: *A human being should live only in harmony with his very own nature and according to his very own nature. He should live in accordance with the truth about himself.*

Pablo's Story

When young Pablo Picasso's
mother noticed him scribbling
all over everything, she provided
him with pencils, colors, and
paper. By age seven he was following his brain's
bent to ultimately produce later art treasures.

What if his mother had punished his earliest
behavior? Or what if she had insisted he take up
a hammer? A violin? A fishing pole?

If a child is exposed early to a variety of
activities and encouraged in the areas he or she
seems to enjoy most, a brain *bent* may begin to
surface. That's why gymnastics and music
lessons, T-ball and chess, golf and art classes (all
in balance, of course) helps the brain develop.
Realizing this, caregivers might object less to all
the running. During such exposures, some
activities are weeded out, while others become
more focused and intentional.

Johnny's parents had him try soccer, but noticed
his frequent excuses to skip practice and even the
games. When it came to saxophone, however, he
had to be coaxed to put the instrument down.
Angie excelled in drama, but was always anxious
for the production to end so she could paint.

In each case, the parents would have been well
advised to invest their time and money in

saxophone lessons and paint pallets—even if all their friends' children *were* playing soccer and performing in plays.

And books! Books should be scattered in playrooms, bathrooms, the car, family room, tree house, porch swing, and kitchen. An alert adult, noticing a child's request for the empty milk carton or a teen's interest in architecture will trot off to the library for craft ideas and design books.

What happens more often is that caregivers only offer experiences that match their own preferences, rather than providing a range of activities. Their thinking: "I like to read, so I'll buy *you* books to read."

Following one's natural brain bent is easier, more fun, and ultimately shapes success. And an adult's calm and neutral openness to a child's interest can help brain bent blossom.

Thomas Alva Edison hinted his opinion on the brain's importance when he wrote:

> *The chief function of your body*
> *is to carry your brain around.*

In your journey toward understanding brain preference, a knowledge of *basic* brain anatomy is mandatory—plus easy, explanatory, and fun! Be sure to read Chapter Three.

Point To Ponder

Your Brain is a sleeping giant. During recent years, researchers in psychology, education, biochemistry, physics, and mathematics have shown that the potential of your brain is far greater than was generally imagined . . . An enormous amount of your capability is still available for development.

—Tony Buzan, in his book
Make the Most of Your Mind

Chapter Three

Anatomy of a Brain *Bent*

"If the human brain were so simple that we could understand it, we would be so simple that we couldn't."

Emerson M. Pugh

Your brain: where is it? Inside a protective bony covering known as the skull. What does it do? Now that's more complicated. This organ, when unimpaired, allows you to remember and reminisce, ponder and plan, meditate and create, invent and solve, daydream and retrace, plot and scheme, feel and emote, envision and celebrate.

What then is it about the brain that is both so intriguing and bewildering? Most people are comfortable talking about their faces and bodies. They pay attention to and pamper their fingers and feet, hair and toenails. Many openly discuss their gallbladder, liver, and heart. Some freely compare notes on procedures that poke, prod, analyze, and even excise.

But the mere mention of one's brain can cause a "curtain to fall; can trigger a person to backpedal into a zone of caution, concern, insecurity—or avoidance. Your brain is, in fact, an amazing three-pound universe. And, like the body, it's composed of many parts.

 By the third week after conception (and some say by the fourth *day* after conception), the brain begins to develop—an organ that can hold 1000 times more information than a twenty-volume encyclopedia. And here's more:

- There are an estimated 100 billion brain cells (neurons) in the human brain, give or take a few billion. That is approximately the number of stars in the Milky Way

- The estimated number of possible synaptic connections in the human brain exceeds the number of atoms in the universe

- A piece of your brain the size of a grain of sand contains 100,000 neurons, two million axons, and one billion synapses

All that in your brain, as unique as your thumbprint!

How Brain Bent Is Built In

Of your brain's many parts, the cerebrum—your thinking brain—is composed of eight lobes, grouped into four divisions by natural fissures. It looks somewhat like this (see diagram below).

According to Benziger, each division has its own built-in scanner. In other words, each section perceives the environment somewhat differently and focuses on specific interests.

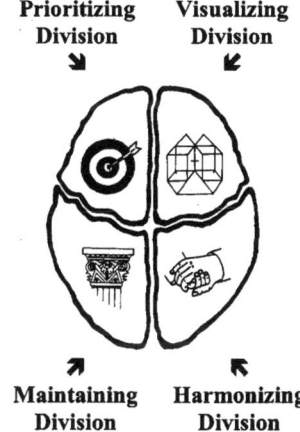

Prioritizing Division

Visualizing Division

Maintaining Division

Harmonizing Division

Stretching the metaphor, think of each division as a specialist in its own field, although there may be some overlap and certainly some collaboration.

The two frontal lobes contain executive functions that enable you to engage in a variety of "executive" activities, so called.

The other six lobes, located behind and slightly below the two frontal lobes, contain decoding centers for sensory stimuli (Visual, Auditory, and Kinesthetic), except for scents or odors, in addition to a whole range of other functions.

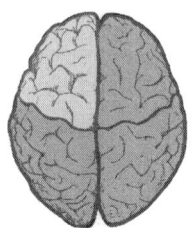 **Examples of Left Frontal Lobe Functions that can help you develop skills related to:**

- Setting and achieving goals
- Making timely and objective decisions
- Engage in inductive/deductive reasoning
- Abstracting and analyzing data
- Managing willpower
- Setting personal boundaries
- Developing and utilizing conscience

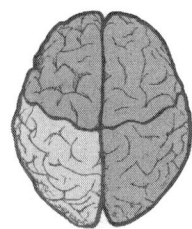 **Examples of Functions of the Left Posterior Lobes that can help you develop skills related to:**

- Following routines accurately
- Implementing activities of self-care
- Honoring and following rituals and traditions
- Learning and following the rules
- Maintaining the status quo
- Providing services necessary to life in society, at work (e.g., activities connected with any service industry), and at home

Examples of Right Frontal Lobe Functions that can help you develop skills related to:

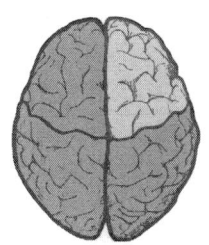

- Anticipating, envisioning, and making changes
- Identifying patterns, trends, and context
- Absorbing the big picture
- Daydreaming and brainstorming
- Risking trying something new
- Enjoying spontaneity
- Honing a sense of humor

Examples of Functions of the Right Posterior Lobes that can help you develop skills related to:

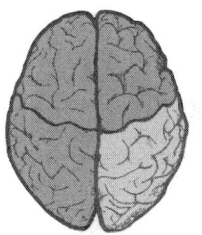

- Promoting connectedness with others and with nature
- Processing spiritual experiences
- Reading nonverbal body language
- Recognizing faces and storing emotional memories
- Honing native music abilities
- Pursuing harmony (e.g., among sounds, colors, shapes, or flavors; with people, nature, and the environment)

While all that anatomical information is interesting, this is what you need to remember: Activities that match your own innate giftedness—your brain's *bent*—tend to require a much lower expenditure of energy.

You have probably heard someone say that buying a certain product (maybe a car?) put a huge dent in his bank account. The carry-over fits. "Bent" rhymes with "dent." And whether you follow your brain's bent (or not!) can result in a smaller or larger *dent* in your energy bank!

Your brain knows how it functions most effectively and wants you to figure this out, too. In a myriad of ways it tries to capture your attention. Sometimes your brain's energy bank "drags its feet" and pushes you to procrastinate.

Sometimes it tempts you to do a favorite activity when you are expected—or scheduled—to do something else. Sometimes it gives you a euphoric burst of energy, or, conversely, allows you to feel irritable, depressed, or even sick.

PET Scans

PET (Positron Emission Tomography) Scans have shown that the brain works many times harder when performing activities that don't match its bent.

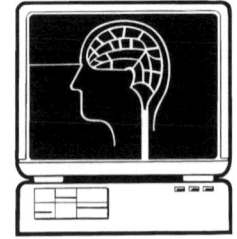

Working "harder" means your brain typically has higher needs for oxygen, glucose, micronutrients, and for a longer recovery time after engaging in activities that don't match its innate energy advantage.

According to Dr. Phil McGraw, in *Self Matters – Creating Your Life from the Inside Out:*

> *Ignoring who you truly, authentically are can literally be killing you . . . Forcing yourself to be someone you are not, or stuffing down who you really are, is incredibly taxing. It will tax you so much that it will shorten your life by years and years . . .*

The secret involves paying attention to your brain's *bent.*

Edison's Story

Thomas Edison, inventor of thousands of patents including the incandescent-light bulb, reportedly said,

> *My mother was the making of me. She understood me. She let me follow my bent.*

Edison's mother, a schoolteacher far ahead of her times, made learning fun. But first she had to remove him from school, where the schoolmaster had called Edison's inattentiveness a form of retardation.

Together she and Thomas did experiments (they called it "exploring") and most people today have the opportunity to sit under light bulbs created by perhaps the most pure inventive genius who ever lived—a grade-school dropout!

How to Get Started

 Figuring out your own brain's bent is a bit like solving a puzzle—the puzzle of *you* and your unique brain.

You can begin by asking yourself several questions:

- What types of activities do you find fun, easy, and energizing?

- What types of activities do you find frustrating, difficult, and exhausting?

- What types of activities are somewhat neutral for you in terms of pleasure, dislike, or energy expenditures?

Once you have a general picture, get more specific and analyze specific activities. Begin by jotting down a dozen or so that you do or are supposed to do on a regular basis. You might find it helpful to begin with your home life, then move on to analyze your work, and finally to evaluate your discretionary (free?) time.

Active versus Passive

Make sure the activities you select require *active* mental picturing versus *passive* mental picturing. Are you aware of the difference?

Active mental picturing is necessary for all types of creativity, problem solving, and brainstorming. Here your brain is actively functioning to accomplish something. For example, building an object with a set of blocks requires the brain to actively design and create.

Passive mental picturing means that your brain is processing what another brain has already actively created. Watching television, for  example, tends to involve more passive mental picturing. That is, you are observing, not performing the activity yourself.

Using passive mental picturing is not all bad. Everyone does it. But it does not challenge the brain and grow dendrites (projections on the neuron much like fingers on a hand), as does active mental picturing.

Knowing up front whether a specific activity is likely to be a good match with your brain bent is a real deal—and a very helpful skill to hone. Engaging in those types of activities will likely put a much smaller dent in your brain's energy bank.

Bent—and Best

What type of brain bent results in the best teacher, minister, doctor, engineer, chef, sales person, secretary, baker—or candlestick maker? The answer is pretty straightforward.

All things being equal, the difference will lie in how easily and energy-efficiently that brain does the key required activities. Almost anyone can select a career and then learn the requisite skills. High achievers in a specific career, however, will likely be those individuals who have a *bent* that matches the key required activities.

When deciding what type of work to pursue, consider these questions:

- How much energy will it take for you to learn the skills needed for key required activities?

- How much energy will it take for you to accomplish the required activities on a daily basis?

- Can you do the required activities well and energy-efficiently, or well but not energy-efficiently?

- How much energy will you have left to devote to social activities and relationships in your personal life?

Warren's Story

Warren's mechanical abilities were known throughout five counties. He had a knack for

finding problems in cars and fixing them reasonably and quickly, and he made big bucks doing just that. However, his first love was teaching. Working on cars bored him, while teaching novice mechanics energized him.

Warren tried to convince his dealership to let him work at the training institute, but they insisted he couldn't be replaced in the garage.

Eventually, Warren left the dealership and started teaching auto-mechanics at a local Community College. Within weeks everyone around him noticed how happier and more energetic he seemed to be.

Keep in mind that individuals with differing brain bents may select similar careers, but will approach them from varying perspectives. They may also achieve different degrees of competence and success based on their innate brain bents.

Your Brain's Bent

Is it possible to match 100% of your life's activities with your brain's *bent*, with the types of activities it does energy-efficiently?

Probably not. It probably would not even be desirable either, because you *do* have a whole brain (assuming you do!) and should use all portions of it—at least some of the time.

A desirable goal is to match a majority (e.g., 51%) of your life's activities with your brain's bent or energy advantage. Just think: more than half of your day, or week, or life spent doing something you love!

Myths and More Myths

Growing up you may have been taught that if something wasn't difficult to accomplish, it probably wasn't worth doing. That's a myth.

Based on emerging brain-function studies, the easier it is for your brain to accomplish a specific activity, and the less energy it requires, the more likely that it's a match with your brain's innate energy advantage..

And then there's the old saying, "If at first you don't succeed, try, try again." In his book, *How the Brain Learns,* Dr. David Sousa writes:

The old adage that "practice makes perfect" is rarely true. It is very possible to practice the same skill repeatedly with no increase in achievement or accuracy of application.

This means you may want to decide if something is *really* worth practicing. If not, then move on to something that is a better match and requires less expenditure of vital brain energy.

The reality is this: A huge difference can exist between what you have learned to do well and what your brain does energy-efficiently. Either your brain is purring along—or lugging behind.

In terms of required energy expenditures, the difference may be as great as pennies on the dollar. *Pennies on the dollar!* Physically, the difference can be energy or exhaustion.

Wave Length Encounters

You've no doubt met people with whom you sensed some brain-connection. You may even have said "We're on the same wave length."

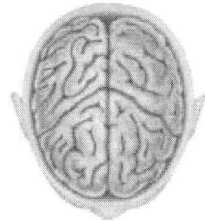 Conversely, you've also met people with whom you sensed no brain-connection whatsoever. In fact, you may even have said something like, "I can't stand to be around that person," or "That person makes my skin crawl."

The latter case can be problematic—especially if you need to work with that individual and/or if you were taught growing up that you were supposed to "love everyone."

Well, listen up. There just may be a brain-explanation for those two diametrically opposed positions. Welcome to the world of neurons and *electromagnetic* or *Em energy*. It has a lot to do with a lot of things.

Em Energy

As you may already know, neurons—cells that have an enhanced ability to transfer information to each other—receive information through finger-like projections known as dendrites.

And the more dendrites you have, the more information you can take in, all things being equal. Neurons send information to other neurons through the axon, the largest projection from each neuron.

Your brain contains upwards of 100 billion neurons. They are believed to form the basis for your IQ or Intelligence Quotient, the potential for which appears to be something you were born with, that you inherit.

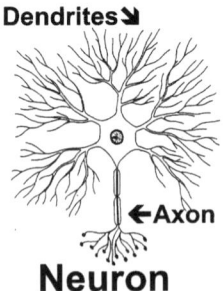

Dendrites↘

←Axon

Neuron

Brain Neurons

In the brain, neurons are thought to be arranged in fields of about a million neurons per field. All neurons in the same field vibrate at the same frequency. They function much as do radio transmitters—sending and receiving their frequency potential and continually discharging electromagnetic energy.

This means that one of the factors that plays into whether you initially "like" or "dislike" another individual, may be based on commonality of neuronal frequency. Just because your brain recognizes some similarities, however, does not necessarily mean it would be a smart move to impulsively invite the other individual into your life. You might want to pay attention to other characteristics he/she exhibits before you make such a decision.

It also means that when you meet another person and your brains recognize no similarities (e.g., you don't sense that "you're on the same wave length"), you may have little if any commonality of neuronal frequency. You can still choose to be gracious and polite in your encounters but you may never select that person to be your closest friend.

Heart Neurons

Did you know that your heart contains neurons, too? Estimates are that at least 40,000 of its cells are neurons that look and function much as do the neurons in your brain. They use the same type of neurotransmitters and are nourished by the same type of neurotrophic food.

Neurons in your heart are thought to form the basis for Emotional Intelligence or EQ, which (you will learn in Chapter Ten) may be far more important to your overall success in life than IQ.

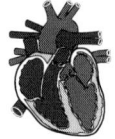 According to Childre and Martin in their book *The HeartMath Solution*, the heart is the most powerful source of electromagnetic energy in the human body. In fact, its neurons may produce Em energy that is 5000 times stronger than that generated by neurons in the brain.

The heart's electromagnetic field extends beyond your body and carries information about your emotional state to people and the environment around you. Energy—a universal, interspecies language, according to Cesar Millan.

In his book *Cesar's Way: The Natural, Everyday Guide to Understanding & Correcting Common Dog Problems,* Millan says: "The most important thing to understand about energy is that it is a language of emotion."

According to Millan, all animals around you (especially pets with whom you share your life) read your energy every moment of every day. His work, especially with canines, has shown how the emotions of an owner can negatively or positively impact the behavior of his/her pet.

If negative emotions can negatively impact one's pet and influence its behaviors, imagine how negative emotions impact people in the same household!

The human body is an electromagnetic field. It both produces and absorbs electromagnetic energy. Electromagnetic energy surrounds and permeates the entire body. Mystics have sometimes referred to this Em energy as the human aura.

This may also help to explain how one very angry or one very cheerful person can impact an entire group of people in a relatively short amount of time. Em energy!

Since every brain is believed to be unique in structure, perception, and function (remember that yours is likely as unique as your thumbprint), your Em energy may be unique as well. It may simply represent another type of *bent*. It's enough to give one pause.

- What type of Em energy is being generated by the people with whom you hang out? How is it impacting you?

- What type of Em energy are you generating? How is it impacting those around you?

A form of radiation energy—much like the rays of the sun—Em energy is believed never to be destroyed. Consequently, generating positive Em energy is a desirable goal since it impacts everything from your brain and body, to your environment and everything it contains (e.g., people, pets, plants)—maybe even the universe, and maybe even forever . . .

Did you know that your mindset can be impacted positively by the amount of exercise you give your brain and body? Studies have shown that for your brain to function at its peak your body needs to move. That's exercise!

John Ratey emphasizes this in his book *Spark,* and describes exactly how and why physical activity is crucial to the way you think and feel:

Aerobic exercise prepares your brain to learn, improves mood and attention, lowers stress and anxiety, helps stave off addiction, controls the sometimes tumultuous effects of hormonal changes, and guards against and even reverses some of the effects of aging on the brain.

Staying True to Oneself

In 1989 Robin Williams starred in the wonderful true story of a college professor named John Keating. *Dead Poet's Society* touched the hearts of many teachers and parents.

In one especially memorable scene, student Neil Perry was chosen for the lead role of Puck in Shakespeare's *Midsummer Night's Dream.* His father, however, a no-nonsense authoritarian, wanted Neil to pursue medicine and forbade him to be in the play.

Neil went to see Keating, his dilemma being whether to conform to his father's wishes or follow his heart's longing. From the book by the same name, the dialogue went like this:

Taking a deep breath Neil said: "My father is making me quit the play . . . Acting is everything to me, Mr. Keating. It's what I want to do!"

"Have you told your father what you just told me? About your passion for acting?" Mr. Keating asked.

"Are you kidding? He'd kill me!"

"Talk to him, Neil," Keating urged.

"Isn't there an easier way?" Neil begged.

"Not if you're going to stay true to yourself."

Staying true to one's self is not always easy, even for adults.

And it can be even harder for teens or young adults whose brains are not yet mature.

More Than Just About My Brain

Marianne Williamson wrote in her book *A Return to Love:*

> *We are all meant to shine . . . And as we let our own light shine, we unconsciously give other people permission to do the same.*

What a concept! Living your own innate giftedness can also free others to do the same. Unfortunately, as Malcolm Forbes put it so clearly,
> *Too many people overvalue what they are not, and undervalue what they are.*

Remember, this is not about whether someone is college educated versus on-the-job trained. This simply says that your heart should partner with your brain.

Heart and brain. Brain and heart.

The ultimate in kindred spirits.

Bent—or dent.

You actually have more control over this than you might think. Identifying and living your brain's innate giftedness by design could conceivably make a positive difference not only in your level of health and happiness but also in your overall success in life.

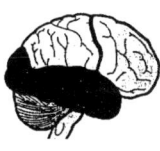

On the other hand, denying your brain's innate giftedness is like barricading future happiness, wellness, and perhaps even longevity.

Maybe Mark Twain's suggestion wasn't all that bad (although it was almost certainly metaphorical if not tongue-in-cheek):

> *You've got to take your brain*
> *out of your head every once in a while*
> *and jump on it.*

Remember: You would be well-advised to match the majority of your life's activities with your brain's innate energy advantage.

Now turn the page to Chapter Four and add the male and female component to brain *bent*. (Talk about energizing!)

Point to Ponder

Men's and women's brains are distinctly different. While men have more neurons in the cerebral cortex (the brain's outer layer), women have more neuropil, which contains the processes allowing cell communication. Neuropil is the stuff between axons, and it is fair to say that, traditionally, it has been largely ignored. Most synaptic activity in the brain occurs in neuropil.

—Gabrielle de Courten-Myers MD,
Associate Professor of Neuropathology at the
University of Cincinnati.

Chapter Four

Calling Planet Earth: the Gender *Bent*

The struggle of the sexes is the motor of history.

Alain Robbe-Grillet Djinn

Men are from Mars and women from Venus. Truth, or myth? Actually some of both, although the way in which men and women sometimes react to each other, you'd think they were from different planets.

In reality men are from Earth—and women are from Earth, too! So it behooves us all to get along right here, right now.

Based on your gender, you will tend to have some built-in brain advantages. Many cultures stereotypically reward each gender for thinking and behaving in specific ways. It can be uncomfortable, even difficult, for individuals whose thought patterns and exhibited behaviors differ from expectations.

Again, understanding how your own brain functions is important in the bigger scheme of things.

Why do gender brain differences matter? Because for those who interact with members of the opposite gender on a regular basis, a communication glitch or misunderstanding based on gender differences can quickly escalate from a mild skirmish into all out war.

Simple spat or blow-out battle, either one is an unfortunate waste of time and vital energy.

Current research shows that neither males nor females know much about each other's brain uniqueness. And the problem goes as far back as human history. As one father said to his daughter when he was reading aloud the story of Adam and Eve: "You know, honey, the problem was not with the apple in the tree as much as with the pair on the ground."

Caution: It is important to avoid ascribing specific characteristics to an entire gender based on an in-depth understanding of one male or one female. Some so-called gender differences may relate more to other factors (e.g., extroversion-introversion preference, sensory system preference, thinking style preferences, strong beliefs or expectations) than to gender.

Saying male and female brains are different simply means that they are unlike. It does not imply good or bad, desirable or undesirable, and certainly not equal or unequal.

Generalizations and Caveats

Much of what is known about brain gender differences comes from a variety of research methods including surveys, questionnaires, direct observation, physical measurements, autopsies, blood tests, and brain scans.

The results of these projects are presented as generalizations—conclusions that commonly apply to nearly 70% of the population. There are some challenges with generalizations, especially when applied to a specific individual.

For example, studies show that on average males are larger than females. There are males, however, who aren't larger than the average female, and there are females who are larger than most males.

Discovering that a generalization doesn't apply to you in every particular instance or situation doesn't invalidate the research; it does exemplify human individuality.

Mara's Story

They were already nearly an hour late. Mara had hinted for Earl to stop for directions, but he hadn't picked up on her suggestion. Finally, she persuaded him to pull into a service station.

Hopping out, Mara said to the attendant, "We're lost. Can you help us with directions?"

Looking at her, the attendant replied, "If you know where you want to go, probably."

Earl looked out the car window and heaved a big sigh. He hadn't wanted to stop in the first place. This business of stopping to ask directions was not only time-consuming, it was embarrassing, as well. He was *sure* he could find his way—eventually.

Ginni's Story

It was their first cruise. Almost from the instant her feet hit the deck, Ginni had no problem finding her way around the ocean liner. Gerry *could* navigate the floors and halls, but not as quickly nor as easily as his wife. Wisely, Gerry decided just to let her enjoy leading the way. He could avoid spending extra energy trying to figure it out for himself. (What a man!)

Similar stories, different reactions. Both illustrate challenges with generalizations. This means that almost every sentence in this chapter could begin, "*In general* the male brain and some female brains . . . " Or, "*most* female brains and *some* male brains . . . "

Nevertheless, researched generalizations are good places to begin when attempting to better understand gender differences.

Direction Finding and Map Reading

Many male brains are quite adept at finding directions, more so than many female brains. But not all.

Yo, males: Will you admit to getting lost more than once, even with a map?

Hey, females: Does your brain read maps easily, so that you rarely become lost?

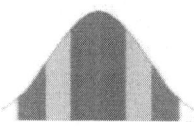

Bell Curve of Distribution

If either of you answered "yes," then you might be in the one-third of the population group who don't match the generalized study conclusion (e.g., fall outside the typical Bell Curve of Distribution that describes two-thirds of the population).

For guys who have trouble reading a map, perhaps you have never been given the opportunity to develop that skill. On your next road trip, choose to navigate—and leave the driving to someone else.

The skills of map reading and direction finding call on functions housed in the two frontal lobes of the thinking-brain layer. Competences related to these functions are developed through exploring-type play during childhood, referred to by Gloria Steinem as "field independence."

Importance of Field Independence

In early childhood, potential abilities for map reading and direction finding are believed to be equally present in the brains of both genders. So what happens after about age eight? In our culture, most little girls have their *field independence* curtailed, usually for safety reasons.

 Little boys, on the other hand, typically are given more field independence. That is, they are allowed to run around more independently and go off exploring on their own. Boys typically can hop on their bikes and take off—if their location and environment permits. They may also congregate down at the corner lot and shoot baskets, wrestle

and rough house, with few restrictions for all types of outdoor activities.

Did that register? The amount of field independence a child experiences can impact ease in direction finding and map reading in adulthood.

Restricted field independence is also associated with a decrease in development of physical abilities, closely connected to developing the visual/spatial skills needed for map reading and finding directions. This is an excellent example of behaviors that may or may not be related to innate ability, but rather are related to skill development built through experience.

Spatial exploration (e.g., climbing trees, building forts, riding bikes, moving the body in space—as in sports) helps both boys and girls. Today's kids should still enjoy these activities. Parents just need to be involved—or stationed close by.

Asking for Directions—A Whole Different Story

While males are generally better at finding directions and reading maps, they are less likely to ask for directions. (Some of you are thinking, *YEAH!*)

One explanation centers on the difference between male and female brains in terms of hierarchical versus collegial organization.

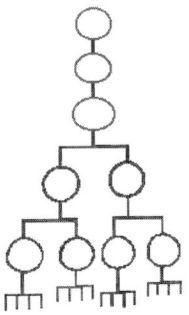

**Hierarchical
Org Chart**

On the hierarchical organizational chart, whoever has the information is perceived as being higher on the pecking order—closer to the top, so to speak.

Because of this perception, asking for information may be perceived by some male brains as an acknowledgement of being at a lower position on the pecking order (at least metaphorically), exactly where most males do not want to be.

How could you solve this in a cross-gender situation?

If you and yours are out looking for the theater and get lost, have the male stop and the female ask for directions. In general, the female brain is interested in the quality of the journey (or experience). To the female way of thinking, asking directions in order to arrive before the show begins will enhance the overall quality of the experience.

Females, on the other hand, tend to think of asking directions as a relational event, rather than as a position on a metaphorical pecking order.

Collegial Org Chart

A collegial organizational chart has fewer levels of pecking-order concerns. In fact, many women who find themselves lost would never think of *not* asking directions. After all, that is the fastest and most efficient way to obtain information, in the female way of thinking.

Nature-Nurture Puzzle

Who you are as an individual member of the human race is determined in large part by the nature-nurture puzzle. In this context, "nature" refers to internal genetic programs that tell the brain how to develop and function in relation to genes, chromosomes, and innate preferences.

"Nurture," on the other hand, refers to external environmental factors that act upon the brain to shape its development. This includes exposure to hormones and other substances or activities during gestation, as well as all the external environmental experiences that occur after birth.

Based on the developmental impact of nature-nurture, plus a host of other factors, each person holds a relative position on what is referred to as the gender continuum. The stereotypical male brain would be at one end of the gender continuum, the quintessential female brain at the other.

According to Baron Simon Cohen, author of *The Essential Difference: The Truth About the Male and Female Brain*, approximately 95% of the population can be placed along the Gender-Brain Continuum.

Note: about 5% of brains will be expected to fall outside the gender continuum.

Gender-Brain Continuum

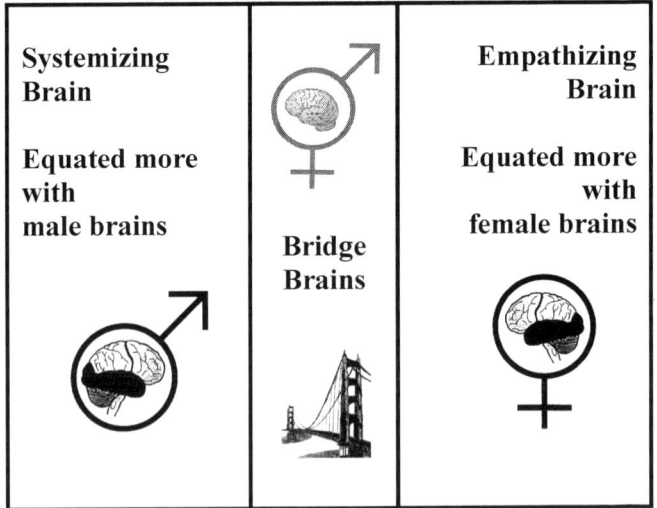

The center position on the gender continuum represents a band of *bridge* brains. This range of "ambigenderity" includes individuals who have 50:50 brains, so called. That is, they possess brain-function characteristics of both genders in almost equal amounts.

Typically, one's brain and body match: a male brain is housed in a male body, a female brain in a female body. (Remember that some individuals may possess a brain that does not match its external housing. For example, a male brain resides in a female body or a female brain resides in a male body.)

Corpus Callosum Bridge

Composed largely of axons, the corpus callosum is the largest of at least three bridges that connect the right and left hemispheres. Studies show differences in the corpus callosum in the male brain versus the female brain, but controversy continues about magnitude and about what those differences really mean. What appears to be consistent is that there are differences.

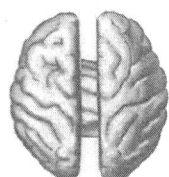 The drawing on the left illustrates the two cerebral hemispheres "pulled apart" a bit so you can "see" the three bridges.

Male Brain

Typically, in the male brain the corpus callosum consists of relatively fewer connecting fibers of a smaller diameter. This probably results both from its gestational chemical bath and from a later onset of puberty. This later puberty onset allows more time for the natural pruning process to occur in the corpus callosum. In fact, it may take up to 1.6 years longer for the male brain to develop its stereotypical *giftedness*.

Note: Research shows that a child who starts taking music lessons prior to the age of seven develops a corpus callosum that is 10-15% larger than that of children who do not take music lessons. If you want the brain of your male child to have a larger corpus callosum, be sure to have him start taking music lessons before the age of seven.

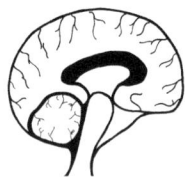

Brain cut-a-way showing a thinner corpus callosum (dark curving band of fibers) in the male brain

Clearly the male brain is designed for what is called lateralized processing: while one part of the male brain is working, the other parts can be idling, so to speak. Consequently, the male brain generally requires less energy to run second for second.

Lateralization also means that the male brain can do two different cognitive tasks at the same time, as long as they utilize functions from separate cerebral hemispheres. Again, one section is working while other sections are idling.

Pete's Story

 Pete is putting together a swing set in his backyard and discussing plans with his wife for a surprise birthday party for their daughter.

However, if Pete tried to assemble the swing set while creating architectural plans for an addition to the garage, it might be a different story since both of those tasks utilize functions from the same hemisphere. In this case he could alternate his attention between working on the swing set and visualizing garage plans. (Or his wife could finish the swing set while he went to work drawing the plans!).

Female Brain

The female brain tends to have a thicker corpus callosum. This likely is due in part at least, to the fact that it did not receive the same type of chemical bath during gestation and because of an earlier onset of puberty. This difference in the corpus callosum is believed to contribute to a more generalized style of processing.

This means that if any part of the female brain is on, it's all on. Consequently, the female brain tends to expend more energy second for second.

Many women excel at multi-tasking because of their ability to rapidly alternate attention from one task to another. In fact, most women can't imagine *not* doing several things at once (even though it actually is very energy intensive for the brain and not nearly as efficient as one might believe).

Brain cut-a-way showing a thicker corpus callosum (dark curving band of fibers) in the female brain

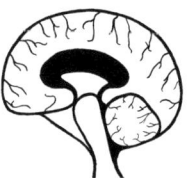

The first part of Maya Angelou's poem *Woman Work* illustrates the multi-tasking exhibited by many women in their daily routine:

> *I've got the children to tend*
> *The clothes to mend*
> *The floor to mop*
> *The food to shop*
> *Then the chicken to fry*
> *The baby to dry*
> *I got company to feed*
> *The garden to weed*
> *I've got the shirts to press*
> *The tots to dress . . .*

Tired yet?

Distractions and the Brain

Studies show that the male brain often concentrates better when there is some distraction in the environment. The opposite is true for the female brain.

For example, in a quiet environment, females tend to score higher on IQ tests—perhaps due to their more generalized style of brain function and because of their increased sensitivity to sounds.

Males, on the other hand, tend to achieve higher IQ scores when there is some distraction in the room. Their more lateralized style of brain function helps them to zero in on the task at hand. It probably doesn't hurt, either, that the male brain is often less sensitive to sounds (e.g., has less acute hearing from birth onward).

Melissa's Story

The hailstorm struck with sudden vengeance. The car was pelted with chunks of ice ranging in size from green peas to green olives. Melissa shook her head and shivered. The sound of ice against metal was overwhelming.

"George," she said to her husband, who had been snoozing in the passenger seat, "are you rested enough to drive? I can't concentrate with all this noise!"

George was and could. They made the change under the next overpass. As the car pulled smoothly onto the highway, Melissa realized that the hail's din didn't seem to faze George. In fact, he was concentrating on the highway so completely that it took Melissa three tries, at one point, to get his attention.

With her more generalized style, Melissa had difficulty blocking out the environmental stimuli and concentrating on driving.

George's more lateralized style found it easier to ignore extraneous stimuli and focus on the task at hand—keeping the car on the road.

Advantages of Generalized Style

Many things in life are neither good nor bad. They do have differing consequences or outcomes. That is, you typically give up something to get something. This seems to be true with the generalized style.

While Melissa's generalized brain had trouble blocking out the environmental noise, her type of brain does have some advantages. Generalized brains tend to react more quickly to an unexpected situation involving both physical and mental stimuli. If a female sees a child fall out of a tree, she may dash to the scene before consciously realizing it.

Typically the female brain excels at tasks that  involve the rapid perception of details and frequent shifts of attention. And, despite myths, females have 14% fewer accidents per miles driven than men.

Generalized reasoning also gives the female brain an edge at long-range planning. But sometimes females are slower at getting the project started.

Advantages of Lateralized Style

In general, the lateralized male brain exhibits a shorter reaction time to a single expected stimulus. This may reflect the goal-oriented, single-mindedness that can occur in a brain with a more lateralized orientation.

Take driving for example. In spite of higher accident rates (which may reflect factors such as exhibition of speed), studies have shown that males actually are better drivers (e.g., more skilled).

As mentioned earlier, the lateralized male brain tends to use less energy second for second. In addition, it can do two different cognitive tasks simultaneously—as long as each task primarily utilizes functions from a separate brain hemisphere.

Barry's Story

Barry pulled his new truck up to the crosswalk line in front of the signal light. To his left sat his cousin Margie in her new red Porsche, engine revving. Barry tooted his horn and gestured toward the red light. Margie nodded. The light turned green and Barry's tires pealed across the intersection a full six feet ahead. Barry was delighted that his truck had beaten a Porsche.

 Barry tended to have faster reaction time to the single stimulus—the green light. However, Barry needs to be especially careful to avoid tailgating in traffic. When it comes to unexpected stops, the female brain often has the edge.

The male brain tends to excel at short-range planning. Males might outline a detailed schedule for next weekend, but likely not for Christmas vacation next year. When they do decide it's necessary, males can take action immediately. They can stop on a dime and get that finger into that proverbial hole in the dyke! *Hmm-m-m.*

Remember:

> *Different does not mean inferior.*
> *Nor superior. Just unlike.*

Trunk or Cabinet? (A Metaphor)

Metaphors, beyond being fun, are useful in understanding comparisons and contrasts. Take the trunk versus the cabinet, for example.

Female Brain as a Trunk

Using this metaphor, the female brain can be compared to a trunk, a place where everything is together in one or two sections. When looking for something in a trunk, this person will bump into other items and can even become distracted from what she was originally looking for.

Tala's Story

One Sunday afternoon Tala, a college coed, was pawing through an old cedar chest, looking for her junior-high journal. Before she got to the journal, she found her favorite childhood doll (later packed for her dorm room). Next Tala uncovered a scrapbook she had put together in fourth grade and became involved in looking at some of the pages and reminiscing.

Then she uncovered her Strawberry Shortcake doll collection, and right after that she located something involving the word "socks" that caused her to shriek with delight.

When asked later about finding her journal, Tala said, "Oh, yeah, I forgot . . . " and headed back up to the attic. Only a "trunk" could have all that fun.

Male Brain as a Cabinet

Compare the male brain, on the other hand, to a cabinet containing many separate drawers, boxes, pigeon holes, and compartments—each with a door or lid. This is one reason the male brain tends to 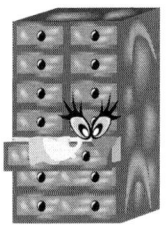 "compartmentalize" (separate) the information being processed. Its style allows it to put something away behind a little door or in a little box and let it simply sit there until the brain chooses to think about it again (or not).

Perhaps because of this, the male brain also tends to adapt easier to working with people that it doesn't like. (That perception is tucked into a compartment, pigeon hole, or drawer and the lid slammed shut.)

Oops . . .

What happens in these two processes? The female brain, much like digging through a trunk, bumps into a variety of information when processing a problem and can become sidetracked.

This style not only may provide additional options to consider, it also can lead to a tendency to integrate, compound, and stew about the newly uncovered information. This could confuse a male brain, however, whose tendency is to avoid addressing an issue that has been tidily "filed" away.

Gender Challenges

Females typically find it more difficult to mentally separate what happens on the job from what happens at home or socially (e.g., that trunk perspective again). If the woman's boss criticizes her work, she is more likely to take the criticism personally. Not, *Your work isn't good,* but rather, *You are no good.* Then she tends to carry the painful criticism home, perhaps even transferring it to the male in the house.

The female brain may also find it more difficult to work with people that it doesn't like—a constant challenge for a generalized brain that keeps bumping into memories or perceptions in that trunk.

Males, with their cabinet perspective, often find it easier to separate criticism of their behaviors from themselves as individuals. "Out of sight, out of mind." This plus can also be a negative for a man who needs some adjustment in thinking or attitude—the challenge for a lateralized brain.

That's why collaboration between genders can be so effective. Stereotypically, males are more goal oriented, females more collegial. Two brains—one male, one female—both being vice presidents in the same company, could help guarantee that the plusses of each brain will contribute positively to long-term success for the organization. A wise administrator will surround him or herself with a variety of brains to insure a balance of contribution.

Calculator and Printout Metaphor

Picture a stereotypical male brain as a calculator with printout capability, and the female brain as a calculator without printout capability. Truth is, if you could cut a thinking-female brain and a thinking-male brain open, you would see similar processes occurring.

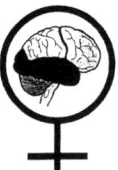 The female, however, who may even arrive at a conclusion more quickly with her generalized style of processing, may find it difficult (if not impossible) to verbalize the sequential steps her brain went through to arrive at the solution because there is no printout capability in her brain.

In the end, a female might be shamed for a perceived lack in this area, and, if pressed, may try to invent "reasons for the reason."

When problem-solving, the male brain tends to function as a calculator, wired with a printout capability. Although it may take longer to arrive at a solution, the male brain can usually identify (metaphorically "print out") the sequential steps his brain went through to arrive at an answer. And, if he wants to, he can articulate these steps.

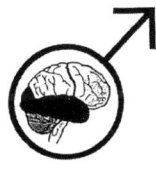 Males who fail to understand that all brains are not equipped with printout capability might discount female answers, when "a sequenced printout" is not forthcoming. Can you perceive how this might be frustrating for both genders?

Using her generalized brain, Mindy suggests a destination when discussing vacation plans. "How did you come up with that?" Steve asks. Mindy explains some of the thoughts that went into her decision (after all she has learned she needs to say something!) but because she finds it difficult to sequentially rehearse the steps her brain went through (as done almost automatically by the male brain), her suggestion is somehow discredited in his eyes.

Imagine the implications in a courtroom setting. Questions are being directed to a female witness: "What gave you the idea that this man was the thief?"

Pause. "I just knew. I had a feeling, a sense . . . "

The jury's female members nod agreement. The male jury members roll their eyes. (Well, maybe not all of them!)

To Shop or Not to Shop—That is the Question

A female brain's tendency to be less goal-oriented and more experience-oriented shows up in a variety of ways. Shopping, for instance!

One man cleverly described the typical gender shopping experience: "Males hunt, women browse." Rarely do cross-gender couples refer to each other as their "favorite shopping partner."

The "experience" of browsing and of comparative shopping thrills the brains of many women (although not all!). Even though car shopping can be comparative, for a man it still becomes more of a hunt that usually involves research and testing.

Sally's Story

When Sally invited her husband, Joe, to accompany her to the mall, he paused for a moment and then asked, "What's on your list?" (Huge clue here, a big red flag regarding brain function.)

Sally, who of course had no written list, scrambled to come up with something plausible. "Uh, I want to look for a peach sweater," she said, "try on some shoes, see what's new this season, and maybe have lunch."

Joe's second question was: "How long do you expect to be gone?" (Alarms should have been sounding in Sally's brain.) Sally, who of course hadn't really thought about how long she would be gone, knew that Joe had no plans for the day. So what did it matter?

In the end, Joe went along. Once at the mall he set out at a brisk pace, leaving Sally behind, and headed directly into the first women's clothing store he saw.

By the time Sally got there (having stopped several times to look at window displays) Joe had rummaged through an entire rack, found a peach (well, really more orange!) sweater and said, "Here. It's on sale. Cross this off your list."

What happened to comparison shopping? The joy of the experience? The companionship Sally had looked forward to? Joe was giving her the gift of a shopping partner, but the male shopping *hunt* is a much different design than two women chitchatting, browsing, wandering around here and there, enjoying the pleasure of being waited on for lunch, and literally killing an afternoon.

For a guy, shopping is generally more goal-oriented, competitive, a little like throwing darts:
Ready . . .
Aim . . .
Fire . . .
Bull's eye . . . Yes!
I'm done!

 For a gal, it's more like eating an ice cream cone—the experience of enjoying the treat matters most, and winning could even mean being the last to finish.

Probably the best that a typical male and a typical female can do when it comes to shopping is to set clear parameters in advance, stick to them, and chuckle about the differences. Or, have him meet her for lunch in the mall. It will save a lot of brain energy for both parties—especially if she's on time.

This is not to say a male brain and a female brain can't shop together in equanimity. Once again, it's all about understanding and choice.

As Milne wrote in *The House at Pooh Corner*:

> *A trifling matter, and fussy of me,*
> *but we all have our little ways.*

The problem is that when it comes to gender relationships, often neither gender thinks their differences amount to a "trifling matter."

Gender Differences and Emotion

Undoubtedly, male or female, you've had a sense of this all along. Studies show that women are more likely to recall emotional events.

Turhan Carili, assistant professor of psychology at State University of New York, Stony Brook, says:

The wiring of emotional experience and the coding of that experience into memory is much more tightly integrated in women than in men.

 The folklore that "husbands never remember marital spats and wives never forget," is now backed up by research. (This study may also shed light on the reason that clinical depression is more commonly diagnosed in women.)

Preliminary research suggests that the amygdalae—brain structures having to do with emotions and memory—grow more quickly in boys than in girls. But males generally don't articulate their deep emotions as frequently or as descriptively as females. Males are much more likely than females to express emotions through actions rather than words. That's why, during a crisis such as the death or illness of a family member or friend, men tend to react by *doing* something rather than by saying something.

A woman might comfort a grieving widow by visiting in her home or by inviting her to lunch; a man might mow her lawn or fix her car. A woman would more likely share sad feelings over an ill child; a man will be on the Internet trying to find cures.

Thinking and Feeling States

Typically, male brains have more difficulty shifting from thinking to feeling states. A classic story from the late 1800s about the differences in gender thinking is *The Revolt of Mother,* by Mary E. Wilkins. It begins with Mother (Sarah Penn) confronting Father:

"Father!"

"What is it?"

"What are them men diggin' over there in the field for?" There was a sudden dropping and enlarging of the lower part of the old man's face, as if some heavy weight had settled therein; he shut his mouth tight, and went on harnessing the great bay mare. He hustled the collar onto her neck with a jerk.

"Father!"

The old man slapped the saddle upon the mare's back.

"Look here, Father, I want to know what them men are diggin' over in the field for, an' I'm goin' to know."

"I wish you'd go into the house, Mother, an' tend to your own affairs," the old man said then. He ran his words together, and his speech was almost as inarticulate as a growl.

But the woman understood; it was her most native tongue. "I ain't goin' into the house till you tell me what them men are doin' over there in the field," said she.

As the story progresses, it turns out that Father is building a barn—another barn—even though Mother has lived for forty years in a house too small, unfinished, shabby, and completely unsuitable for daily living or any sort of entertaining. Their daughter's wedding was coming up and Mother wanted a brand new house. She put it to Adoniram straight:

"You've built sheds an' cow-houses an' one new barn, an' now you're goin' to build anther. Father, I want to know if you think it's right? You're lodgin' your dumb beasts better than you are your own flesh an' blood . . . "

But Adoniram built the barn anyway.

Just days before the cows were to move in, Adoniram Penn had to make an emergency trip. During his three-day absence, Sarah Penn and her two children frantically emptied everything from the little old house and triumphantly moved into the big new barn.

Then Father returned.

"I've made it the subject of prayer an' it's betwixt me an' the Lord. The house wa'n't fit for us to live in any longer, an' I made up my mind I wa'n't goin' t' stay there."

. . . The old man's shoulders heaved: he was weeping. Adoniram was like a fortress whose walls had no active resistance, and went down the instant the right besieging tools were used. [And the kicker--]

"Why, Mother," he said, hoarsely, *"I hadn't no idée you was so set on't as all this comes to."*

No idea?

All those years Adoniram Penn just plain didn't "get it."

His lateralized thinking style drove him toward his goals in a one-track direction, tuning out his wife's needs and pleas. Fortunately, he "got it" before his only family members were his cows!

Hope for Relationship Success

It's time to make more functional decisions about ways to relate to members of both genders.

> *Myth*: "Anything your brain can do, mine can do better."

> *Fact*: "Actually, maybe not. So what?"

The greatest challenge of all is this: to your own gender-brain be true. Celebrate wildly who you are—generalized or lateralized, trunk or cabinet, printout capability or not. Each style is part and parcel of being human.

Does knowing your gender brain preference lock you into functioning in a specific style? No. It can help you to realize why you tend to expend more energy and perhaps be less successful when consistently employing your brain in a manner that doesn't match its innate strengths.

Understanding your gender brain and recognizing similarities and differences of your closest loved ones or work associates can enhance relationships in a way you might not have dreamed possible. Of course, merely knowing the differences doesn't remove them.

It does provide more options. It can also empower you to identify those options and make collaborative choices that honor differences without taking them personally. Or by allowing gender differences to interfere with achieving positive outcomes.

Understanding more about gender-differences and the brain sets one free to select (by design) a more effective behavior in specific situations.

Remember: *different* does not mean inferior. Nor superior. Just *unlike.*

Are you getting that? It took poor old Adoniram forty years. Most people could probably do much better than that—if they chose to.

A Final Note on Gender Brain Preference

Dame Ivy Compton-Burnett (1884-1969) said:

> *There is more difference within the
> sexes than between them.*

That was a pretty radical insight for her time!

Societal myths have caused many to investigate their strengths rather reluctantly, quite simply because they do not believe their natural talents fit the expectations. It may not be easy to be female and excel in math or debate. It may be somewhat uncomfortable to be male and excel in connecting or nurturing. Nevertheless, if it's your brain's innate giftedness, go for it!

Respect

Deep inside one's psyche is a need to be viewed as an individual worthy of respect, a need so powerful many have risked life and limb to fulfill it.

 In all interactions, from playground squabbles to the establishment of families to the corporate boardroom, it is important to learn to treat people with respect.

For increased effectiveness, long-term health and happiness, and to make the contribution that only you can bring to this world, remember the words of Martin Buber:

Every person born into this world represents something new, something that never existed before. It is the duty of every person to know that there has never been anyone like her/him in the world, for if there had been, there would be no need to be.

"Every person born into this world" includes *you*, of course.

The next chapter continues that idea of individual uniqueness into the world of environmental comfort zones. Turn the page.

Point To Ponder

I believe it benefits almost everyone to know as much as possible about how his/her own brain works.

—Daniel G. Amen MD

Chapter Five

I'm Okay. What's Your Problem? The *Bent* of Extremes

*How glorious it is—and how painful also—
to be an exception.*

Alfred de Musset, 1857

No doubt Michael was the quietest student Mrs. Tanner had ever taught in her twenty-year career. Placed in her class for both seventh- and eighth-grade English, he appeared unusually and painfully shy. While his work was always turned in on time, this teacher barely knew the sound of his voice. Michael worked alone, spent free time alone, and ate alone. But this is not to say that he appeared unhappy or depressed. He actually had a pleasant face and smiled often, but mostly to himself.

When Michael completed eighth grade, Mrs. Tanner worried about how life would go for him in high school, where loud and crazy ruled. She rarely saw him after that and, of course, Michael wasn't the type to return for a visit.

At the extreme opposite, meet Dolly. Her piercingly shrill—as many described it—voice was the first to be heard in the morning (often after the opening bell!) and the last in the afternoon. Dolly, rarely alone, was in the middle of everything happening in the schoolroom or on the playground. She was noisy, fidgety, and, at times, argumentative.

It's no surprise that Dolly and Michael rubbed each other wrong: like cats and dogs, oil and water, introverts and extraverts (sometimes spelled extroverts). It happens all the time— unless people really understand something about brain function and the resulting differences in behavior that can be triggered by differing brain function.

Some tend to think their style of brain-function is the norm. For example, notice the differences in perception by the following two authors:

- Written from an extraverted perspective:

  People who make no noise are dangerous. —J. de LaFontaine, *Fable,* 1678

- Written from an introverted perspective:

  Noise is the most impertinent of all forms of interruptions. —A. Schopnhauer, 1852

Extroversion, Ambiversion, and Introversion

From childhood, many people develop stereotypical beliefs about the term *introverted.* You may have heard these individuals described as shy, retiring, loner, hard-to-get-to-know, stuck up, or even "wall flower."

What about the term *extraverted?* Try descriptions such as outgoing, lively, in-the-public-eye, life of the party, overactive, fidgety, noisy, or class clown.

In suggests inward; *ex,* outward. And so there are counterparts of attention—one directed within the self (introversion), the other directed outside the self (extraversion).

Add to that *ambi*, which suggests parts of both, forming the basis for the less-familiar word *ambiversion.* It describes the state of being neither extremely extraverted nor extremely introverted, but expressing aspects of both.

These differing states are sometimes expressed as a continuum: extreme extraversion (E) at one end, extreme introversion (I) at the other, and ambiversion (A) in the middle. Every human being is believed to reside innately somewhere on this continuum (although each can also move along the continuum based on what is required in the environment at any given moment).

EAI Continuum

One's relative position on the EAI Continuum (see drawing below) may be as vital to one's sense of self as one's innate brain *bent*. Carl Jung, renowned Swiss psychologist and researcher, certainly thought so. Since these terms really describe *environmental comfort zones,* perhaps a person *does* need to sustain a comfortable level of stimulation before he/she can fully engage in thinking functions.

Extreme Extraverts	Ambiverts	Extreme Introverts
E = 15%	A = 70%	I = 15%

Depending on your innate position on the EAI Continuum, your brain will function most effectively and feel more alive, alert, and energetic in a specific type of environment—one that offers a great deal of stimulation (E), one with moderate stimulation (A), or one with little stimulation and providing protection from over-stimulation (I).

How have others described you regarding this perspective? Do you consider yourself extraverted, ambiverted, or introverted? Perhaps at times, you have sensed that a specific environment was not a good fit for you. For example, a group was too quiet for your tastes, or a party was way too loud.

Can you already identify environments in which you feel comfortable versus those that you prefer to avoid at all costs? What about environments where you can survive or enjoy for a short period of time, but then just *have to get out of there*? Figuring out your own preferred position on the EAI Continuum can be like discovering buried gold.

It can be helpful to think of this concept in terms of three differing types of brains. (It's not quite that simple—nothing ever is—but this should work for our purposes.)

Extraverted Brain

This brain has high needs for stimulation and low needs for relief from stimulation. We often refer to this type of brain (or person) as being extremely extraverted. About 15% of the population falls into this category.

These brains (people) gravitate toward stimulating environments that may, or may not, involve people. Some extraverts prefer to obtain stimulation from sources other than people (e.g., computer games, sports, high-risk activities).

Those with extremely extraverted brains often perform better (socially, physically, or academically) under pressure or in the face of competition because of the added stimulation these situations provide.

In effect, the stimulation serves to *wake up* their brains. Without sufficient amounts of stimulation, they may become restless, bored, and literally feel sleepy.

Ambiverted Brain

This type of brain has relatively equal needs for stimulation versus relief from stimulation. Estimates are that approximately 70% of the population falls into this ambiversion range.

These brains (people) are neither extremely extraverted nor extremely introverted. Sometimes they crave stimulation; sometimes they need relief from stimulation. Time spent in stimulating environments, however enjoyable, needs to be compensated for with recovery time spent in environments much less stimulating.

Introverted Brain

The introverted brain has low needs for stimulation and high needs for relief from stimulation. These brains (people) actually need to be protected at times. We usually refer to this type of brain as being extremely introverted. Roughly 15% of the population falls into this category.

When this type of brain becomes over-stimulated, it tries to shut out further input, but that does not mean it literally shuts down.

Rather, introverts retreat internally, almost automatically, to block out additional stimuli while they evaluate, process, search for insight, and reflect on what's been going on.

These individuals may perform less well under the pressure of exams, conflict, high-risk activities, or competition because of the high level of stimulation inherent in those situations.

Part of the Package

Just as gender brain preference is in place when you "come out of the chute," you are believed to arrive with your own innate position on the EAI Continuum already assigned. Personnel who have spent years working with newborns, infants, or toddlers have reported they can often identify the extremes of extraversion or introversion quite quickly, sometimes within days of birth.

If you are a parent of an *extreme*, you might have researched this in your own personal laboratory—your home.

An infant with an extremely extraverted brain may sleep fewer hours (although not always), may stop crying only when passed around the room to a dozen different caregivers, and may rattle the crib or bang its head on the bed frame in an effort to obtain stimulation.

Some of you might be saying right now, *Yes, I tore my hair out with just such an extraverted child. She was always getting into some type of mischief.* Obviously looking for stimulation!

An infant with an extremely introverted brain may sleep longer hours and may stop crying only when placed in a quiet, darkened room. Or perhaps will go to sleep only when allowed to lie quietly instead of being rocked.

This type of child is more likely to become ill when over-stimulated. Parents of this child (especially if it is the firstborn) might have thought, "Piece of cake. Let's have more!" only to discover that the second child's brain was very different in terms of placement on the EAI continuum (e.g., ambiverted or extraverted).

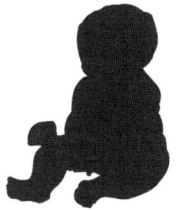

On the other hand, an extremely extraverted parent might have thought something was wrong, their introverted child being so different from the parent.

The majority of children fall within the range of Ambiversion. They have more balanced needs for stimulation and for relief from stimulation. Identifying one's position in the ambiversion range occurs by exclusion—that is, if the child is neither extremely extraverted nor extremely introverted, then he or she likely falls in the ambiverted range.

A caregiver's job is to figure out what that child's brain craves in terms of stimulation and under what circumstances. Then help the child understand which environments are optimum and which can be more stressful.

It can get a little worrisome when your two-year-old goes into the bedroom and shuts the door or hides behind the couch. At the same time, it is exhausting when your two-year-old never wants to play alone. And, if not enough is going on, decides to take matters into his/her own hands.

Of course life with toddlers (or teens!) can be exhausting with any brain preference. However, understanding some of these factors can make all the difference in the world in terms of one's responses. Especially in the face of a human tendency to think that there is something *wrong* with another brain when it doesn't *think* or *act* like yours does.

Societal Rewards Have Changed

In Europe, during the Middle Ages, introversion was generally valued over extroversion. That is, individuals with a brain bent toward introversion were often rewarded over a brain bent toward extroversion.

Those with extremely introverted brains often gravitated to a religious order—a high honor in that society or culture.

Away from the hustle and bustle of materialism, they found solitude and validation for their abilities to study, copy the scriptures or other books, write, compose, or illustrate. Some found this environment conducive to developing a spiritual connection with a higher power.

As the shift toward industrialization occurred, extraversion rose in favor. As religious orders became secularized, fewer protected environments were made available for those who were extremely introverted.

In any event, today's society doesn't deal effectively with either extreme—extraversion or introversion. Extremely extraverted children are often punished and/or medicated, in an effort to dampen their stimulation-seeking behaviors.

Extremely introverted children are often pushed toward competition and/or punished for a perceived lack of participation. Introverted teenagers may be mocked, shunned, or excluded, since they are too quiet or perhaps too withdrawn for other students to get to know.

As adults, extremely extraverted males may get by easier than extremely extraverted females who don't meet societal expectation for "nice" women. Neither gender is rewarded for being extremely introverted, although an introverted female might have an easier time—possibly being viewed as more "feminine."

Camera Metaphor

Imagine that each brain has its own camera with a uniquely sized aperture. If the opening to the brain's "camera" is relatively small, that brain needs to take lots of pictures to obtain the required stimulation. Much action and input is needed—and if not readily available, the individual will create his or her own. These extraverted brains may even self-medicate with chemical stimulates such as caffeine.

If the brain's "camera" has a large aperture, it can take in huge amounts of data second for second and become quickly overloaded and over-stimulated. A very active environment can be overwhelming for an introverted brain.

If the brain's camera has a moderate aperture, individuals who are ambiverted have nearly equal needs for stimulation and for relief from stimulation.

Differing Apertures

When Alfred de Musset said, "How glorious it is—and how painful also—to be an exception," he reminds us that there is a certain discomfort—or a certain glory—in being unique. Both the pain and the glory of extreme extraversion and extreme introversion represent two specific types of giftedness.

Each can thrive in the appropriate environment. For example:

- Extreme extraverts are often able to function very effectively in situations that would almost immobilize an extreme introvert and be difficult for an ambivert

- Extreme introverts can process information internally or in secluded (even isolated) environments that would put an extreme extravert to sleep and, again, can be difficult for an ambivert

Extreme Extraversion

Extreme extraverts are great participators (although not necessarily great team players). They are more likely to engage in a good debate or roughhousing. They tend to have excellent short-term memory, but may also forget things more quickly. If they read, it's often to gain additional stimulation. On the other hand, if there's enough going on in the environment to give them their needed level of stimulation, they may avoid reading altogether.

Extreme extraverts tend to score higher on positive mood scales. That means they might seem happier than introverts, perhaps because they are less introspective. They are also more likely to get into trouble in school, especially if the specific classroom is geared for the more introverted brain—which many classrooms are.

When these extraverts are not getting enough stimulation, they can become quickly bored and may even fall asleep—if they haven't already gotten into trouble during their search for stimulation.

They can excel at activities that would be virtually impossible for extreme introverts: negotiating in situations of high-tension, competing under situations of high stress, participating on a SWAT team. Their extreme giftedness pulls them through.

In S. E. Hinton's book *The Outsiders*, we are introduced to gang members from both sides of town: the Socs (Socials) and the Greasers. As Ponyboy narrates the story, he describes his Greaser-gang friends. One stands out—Two Bit, the "wisecracker of the bunch." Here is a classic description of an extreme extravert:

"[Two Bit] couldn't stop making funny remarks to save his life. You couldn't shut up that guy . . . Life was one big joke to Two Bit . . . He was always smarting off to the cops. He really couldn't help it. [Regarding school] He just went for kicks."

Ever go to school or work with someone like that? Or, was that someone you?

Extreme Introversion

Extreme introverts tend to be life's observers.
You may see them sitting or standing alone.
They may go off and take a walk or nap when
things around them get too busy. They may like
people but they usually prefer to take them in
very small groups, or on a one-on-one basis.

They often enjoy face-to-face conversation when
the subject is of interest to them, but often they
would just as soon use e-mail. They tend to do
better at the university level where there is more
opportunity for independent study.
Unfortunately, an extreme introvert can feel like
a misfit in today's society.

Jared's Story

Jared did feel like a misfit. Not just in society,
but even in his own home! For as far back as he
could remember he'd always been at odds with
the other three members of his family. Oh, they
loved each other. They really did. But they
definitely didn't understand each other. They
were in a constant tug of war.

It would go like this: "Come on, Jared. Let's go
have a game of basketball."

When Jared invariably replied, "You go ahead, I
think I'll stay here and work on the computer,"
someone was sure to climb his frame, all six feet

of it! His parents and younger brother wondered why he didn't want to do things with them, and why he was so often sick, which meant he *couldn't* participate.

Jared's extremely introverted brain was simply trying to grow up in an environment orchestrated by three extreme extraverts. The poor chap was dying from too much stimulation. No wonder he was sick so much of the time.

Classic Introvert

Emily Dickinson was most likely a classic introvert. She kept herself secluded behind closed doors for years. But her mind was beyond active.

Dickinson revealed, through her letters and poetry (see lines below) not only an introverted brain, but also a brain wanting recognition, a person anxious to be revealed and accepted on her own terms.

The soul selects her own society,
Then shuts the door;
On her divine majority
Obtrude no more. [. . .]
I've known her from an ample nation
Choose one;
Then close the valves of her attention
Like stone.

Harold's Story

Upon graduation from high school, Harold got a summer job selling children's home-library books door-to-door. It was a good opportunity to earn a major portion of his college tuition, so he applied himself to the task and worked very long hours. Sales were slow, however, and Harold was near exhaustion and burnout. He had trouble facing rejection, especially when it was meted out even before he could display his wonderful books. Many days he simply could not face knocking on the first door. Discouragement was moving toward depression. He was done—college tuition or not.

Fortunately, Harold found another job as an equipment operator on a highway construction project. The job required twelve-hour days, but the work seemed like play compared to sales. Several years later, this young man attended a brain-function seminar and discovered that extreme introversion and door-to-door sales are usually incompatible matches, regardless of the person's age, the product's quality, or even personal desire.

How affirming for Harold to realize that his *lack of success* (some of his friends called it outright failure) as a salesperson wasn't due to lack of purpose, nor to some defect in his character. The activity was simply too energy-exhausting for his highly introverted brain.

Can you imagine an extreme extravert doing computer programming in a cubicle, composing music in a solitary studio, doing research in a one-person lab, or working as a bookkeeper? What about an extreme introvert working as a negotiator, running a small retail business and trying to be all things to all customers, selling advertising, practicing as courtroom attorney in high-profile cases, or trying to succeed as a telemarketer? Imagine how exhausting and painful for an introverted brain.

Mark's Story

Mark was in high demand. The leaders of his denomination considered him to be one of their finest and most inspirational speakers. And his dozen-plus books had topped the charts in sales. For years he had been a traveling evangelist, but when he finally accepted a job as senior pastor for a large university-affiliated church, the congregation was thrilled. Week after week, Mark delivered inspiring, thought-provoking, and exquisitely crafted homilies.

Each week, when the sermon concluded, Mark (like Elvis) would disappear. People wanted to shake his hand and thump his back, but he was gone! Finally the congregation, choosing to be offended by what they perceived to be Mark's rude social behaviors, approached the church board. This guy isn't a pastor," they complained. "He hardly even speaks to us."

It was true. Mark was not a typical pastor, certainly not the type that many congregations have come to expect. His was an extremely introverted brain.

Being in front of the podium put him in a one-to-one situation with the congregation. Not a problem.

 Take him out of the podium and put him in the midst of a large group of people, however, and his eyes would glaze over. He would freeze.

The congregation needed to decide whether they wanted a fantastic preacher or a stereotypical pastor.

After seemingly endless meetings, the church board finally concluded that there were other individuals on staff who could shake hands at the door, make house visits, and show up at potlucks and picnics. They'd keep their senior pastor, enjoy his talents, and give him his space.

Bravo! Would that other organizations studied brain function by design, with the purpose of helping their employees succeed. It's definitely "different strokes for different folks," and all types are needed to make for a successful community.

They're Everywhere!

It's not just pastors. Similar stories are rumored about famous actors and actresses. On stage or in front of the camera, these often highly-introverted individuals are outgoing, clownish, and brilliant with repartee. Backstage they are loners.

Take Johnny Carson, for example. When he retired, he disappeared! Others with highly introverted brains have chosen to live in seclusion (some on a tiny island) and interact with the outside world only as absolutely necessary for their profession. How they are misunderstood! How often their adoring public rakes them over the proverbial coals when requests for autographs and interviews are ignored, avoided, or declined less than gracefully.

Kurt Vonnegut's story, *Who Am I This Time?* (later made into a film) illustrates the special giftedness of an extreme introvert, Harry Nash.

 Harry could not even hold a *decent* conversation with people he had known forever. On the stage, however, he could powerfully assume almost any role: Abraham Lincoln, Julius Caesar, Cyrano de Bergerac, Socrates . . .

93

Harry literally *became* the person he was playing. But when the play was over, even before the final bows, Harry was gone.

One high school drama coach remarked that she used to invite the outgoing, extraverted students to try out for plays, assuming they would have a natural bent for being out in front. Instead, she discovered that many of those kids were absolutely terrified to be on stage. Absolutely terrified!

One day, strictly by accident, she mentioned to a very introverted junior that he might want to try out for the upcoming play, *The Importance of Being Ernest*. Surprisingly, he said, "Okay." At tryouts he shocked everybody, including himself, with an amazing interpretation—and ended up with the lead.

At the performance, he knocked everyone's socks off. But after the performance, when it was time for punch and cookies, the student-actor was nowhere to be found.

Callus or No Callus

Think back to individuals you have known who likely had extremely introverted brains. Did they appear overly sensitive? Were you afraid to hurt their feelings? Were they difficult to get to know?

Conversely, think of those you've known who likely had extremely extraverted brains. At school, at home, even at work you probably could do everything short of saying, "Sit still and shut up!" and nothing slowed them down. They were so busy searching for the stimulation their brains craved that they rarely stopped to think about the consequences. What do you think they got for the laughs and the attention? More stimulation!

You might want to picture the extremely extraverted brain as having a type of callus (hard and thick) that protects it from being readily hurt or bested in highly stimulating, competitive, or combative situations.

Individuals with this callus thrive in scenarios that could decimate brains that don't posses such a protection. Carpenters sometimes develop a callus on their skin to protect from slivers. String players develop them on their fingers to allow them to play the instrument without pain.

For extremely introverted brains, however, there is no such callus. Too much stimulation and they become overloaded quickly. They may feel pain, become sick, or shut down—often by distancing themselves from the stimulating environment.

Porcupine was the nickname I gave this chestnut burr, and thought it very appropriate.
—Natsume Soseki, Botchyan

This is like the proverbial "people-are-eggs" idea. Some extreme introverts withdraw from the group, even at the risk of being labeled stuck up. For them, being alone is safer than being teased, laughed at, or pushed to participate—especially when competition is involved.

Have you ever asked someone to play a game of table tennis and the first thing out of the player's mouth was, "Do we have to keep score?" Likely an extreme introvert. Have you ever suggested just playing for fun, and had an extreme extravert comment, "What's the point of playing if we're not going to keep score?"

Different responses to a similar situation: neither good nor bad. Not desirable or undesirable. Just unlike. It helps to understand.

Cats Don't Bark

How much more effective life could be if culture and society stopped putting so much pressure on its members to conform to a "one size fits all." Being different is okay. It's not only okay it's the way life is. After all, we wouldn't expect a cat to bark or a dog to fly.

Speaking of animals, some cats are introverts—they ignore you, hide under the rocking chair, and turn their backs on the one who feeds them. And yet we love those people-tolerating felines anyway and *because* . . .

Some attention-begging dogs are extreme people-lovin' extraverts, and we love them anyway and *because*, as well.

How is it that we find it so much more difficult to love people *because*? There is such a tendency to love human beings not *because* but *although* or *in spite of* . . .

The Challenge

Identify the context (environment) in which your brain operates most efficiently. Cut some slack to the differences between a brain that tolerates or craves huge amounts of stimulation, versus one that doesn't need or cannot tolerate high levels of stimulation, or the one that needs a balanced blend of both. Notice the changes this can make in your world, personally as well as professionally.

It's all about valuing the innate uniqueness and giftedness of each individual. Remember that you will likely be much more successful if you identify your approximate position on the EAI Continuum and match the majority of your activities to your brain's own unique need for stimulation or for relief from stimulation.

Let's to back to Mrs. Tanner's junior high English student from years ago. When Michael graduated from high school, he contacted his former teacher.

Stopping by the school, he entered her classroom and handed her a pencil-written, two-sided note that read:

 *Thanks for letting me be me. Even though I was quiet, I learned a lot. I'm not really as shy as everyone thinks.*

Of course he wasn't *shy*. No more than the shyness each of us experiences in a new or unfamiliar situation. He did have an extremely introverted brain, however, which is an entirely different matter.

Now, with studies from advanced brain research available, Mrs. Tanner could have validated this student's giftedness as an extreme introvert with much greater relevance, acceptance, and enthusiasm. Years later she learned that Michael was making his mark as a noted researcher. Thank goodness for people like that.

We each know individuals who remind us of Dolly and Michael. As you think about people you have met who fall into the category of either extreme extraversion or extreme introversion, you may recall times when you might have misunderstood them. You may even feel reflective, or regretful, about the way in which you responded to or ignored them. Most likely you hadn't the least idea of what was actually going on in their respective brains.

Often, with the right touch from a sensitive person, an introvert will exercise rare moments of extraversion. Or perhaps the most glaring extravert will surprise even best friends with profoundly serious thoughts and deep feelings.

That's all part of the gold and part of the glory.

In *Self Reliance*, Ralph Waldo Emerson wrote:

> *For nonconformity the world*
> *whips you with its displeasure.*

And that *whipping* for nonconformity can come in any number of differing ways, from any number of differing sources, and in any number of differing environments. Frightening!

Done any whipping lately?

Been whipped?

In today's world, teachers, parents, neighbors, bosses, co-workers, partners—all humans—are not only challenged but also obligated to do away with inappropriate stereotyping.

> *We do better when we know better.*
> *Now we know better.*

Next, differences include another component: Sensory Preference. Savor Chapter Five.

Point To Ponder

There are those who will call you a recluse—
but it is better to listen to your own different
drummer than to go through life with
a ringing in your ears.

—William Safire, *On Language*

Chapter Six

A Sense in Time Saves Mine—the Sensory *Bent*

*As your senses awaken, all the inlets
to the mind are set open.*

—Cathleen Schine, *Rameau's Niece*

Your brain impacts your internal world by playing a key role in creating perceptions, beliefs, reactions, opinions, responses, feelings, and behaviors. It also influences your interactions with the external world. And that means your senses.

Think about a gift you would love to receive:

- Perfume or cologne (scent)

- A box of candy or fruit (taste)

- A theater ticket (sight and sound)

- A music CD or a ticket to a musical concert (hearing and sight)

- A comfy outfit of your choice (touch)

- A sculpture or painting (sight)

- A gift certificate to your favorite restaurant (taste if the food is wonderful, visual if it has lovely décor, and even auditory if you like the ambient music)

- A DVD (sight, perhaps sound, and . . . touch if you're snuggled up to a friend or a pet while you view it)

Do you have preferences for one of these (or for something similar) based on your preference for seeing, hearing, or sensing kinesthetically? Many people do.

Sensory Preference

Most humans are believed to have a sensory preference—that is, one type of sensory stimuli tends to register more quickly and intensely in their brain. You typically are more comfortable receiving sensory data in your preferred system and likely do so with less expenditure of energy.

Also, when communicating with others who have a similar sensory preference you may feel better understood. In addition, understanding some of the characteristics typically exhibited by individuals based on their sensory preference can help you deal more effectively with others.

This may be a good time for you to complete the *Sensory Preference Assessment* (see Appendix A). Share it with your family members, close friends, and coworkers. The results may verify what you already know or give you a surprise. You may learn something very valuable about yourself. Even if you think you already know your sensory preference, perceiving that information on paper can be immensely helpful.

The senses are often described in terms of three main groupings: the Visual System, the Auditory system, and the Kinesthetic system. Identifying your sensory preference doesn't mean that you only use that sensory system. It does mean that those types of stimuli tend to register most quickly and intensely in your brain.

Understanding Your Sensory Preference

Sensory stimuli—the information absorbed through eyes, ears, nose, mouth, and skin—tend to get your attention. You relate to others and the environment through your senses. Unless you have altered perception in one of the sensory systems (e.g., sight or hearing impaired, altered sense of smell), you tend to use all of the senses to decode sensory data that comes to your brain.

You may be aware of one system more than another in specific situations, as well. For example, you may be more aware of your Auditory system when attending a musical concert, your Kinesthetic system while eating a holiday dinner, or your Visual system when traveling to a new country or when watching a movie.

If you visit a friend who lights a candle before you show up (knowing you love the scent or sight), you feel honored. Maybe another friend always includes crackers and cheese on the table, knowing your sensory preference of taste. If your preference is Auditory, friends might have the stereo playing one of your favorite selections or might take you to a concert of your favorite music. In each case, you may experience a sense of ease, comfort, and pleasure because of the match with your brain's sensory preference.

All There from the Beginning . . .

Sensory preference is thought to be innate and may be observable very early (e.g., some fetuses have been seen sucking a finger on imaging tests and they may be Kinesthetic). Personnel who work in newborn nurseries may be able guess a baby's sensory preference based on watching the infant. For example, some infants (far more than others) like to touch the satin edging on blankets and seem to be more bothered by rough textures or wrinkles in the linen. Kinesthetic? Some infants want to see everything and don't like to have their bassinette's covered. Visual? And some infants are very sensitive to sounds. Auditory?

Adults who work with children and who understand sensory preference can often identify a child's sensory preference by the age of five or six. Sensory preference probably won't change much in adulthood, unless the individual was shamed or abused during childhood in a way that prompted him or her to repress, deny, or ignore sensory preference.

You likely take in information more easily and energy-efficiently when it comes to you in your sensory preference.

Communication involves the sensory systems in some way or another. Simply by understanding more about the sensory systems in general and becoming more aware of your preference as compared to others, you can enhance all your relationships.

Matching Gifts with Preference

Interestingly enough, many people buy gifts for others based on their own sensory preference—rather than matching the gift to the other person's sensory preference. You may think, *I love books, so I'll buy my friend a book.* Or, *I like music so I'll give my friend a CD.* Or, *This scarf style is all the rage right now so I'll purchase a scarf as a gift.* Hmm-m-m. If your friend is Kinesthetic you might be better to give a gift certificate so the person can be certain it "feels right" before the purchase.

Here's an example of how the sensory preference of a loved one can apply to demonstrating your affection. Let's say your daughter Mellie is at college in another state. You want to communicate how much you love and miss her.

If Mellie is a Visual, you might send her a gift for her dormitory room—a plant, picture, poster, or flower arrangement. Remember to tell her often how beautiful she is, how much you like the décor in her room, or how much you miss *seeing* her around the house.

On the other hand, if Mellie is an Auditory, you could send her a CD, wind chimes, or an e-mail song-card. Tell her often that you look forward to hearing the sound of her voice. Give her a calling card or cell phone minutes so she can phone home often.

If Mellie's *bent* is towards being Kinesthetic, she might enjoy a cuddly teddy bear, a soft quilt or feather pillow, scented candles, or a health club membership. When you're together, give her a hug or treat her to her favorite activity—tennis, a massage, swimming, or hiking.

Similar types of sensory-matched gift ideas work equally well for your spouse, partner, or best friend. Learning about sensory preferences can empower you as an individual and it can also extend beneficially into your family, school, social, church, and work worlds.

Remember, human beings tend to return to environments in which they feel comfortable—environments that they perceive to be nurturing, validating, and accepting. They typically make such a determination based on their own sensory preference and whether or not it is honored and provided for in a specific environment.

Brain Layers

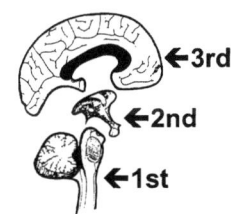

To simplify, view the brain as being composed of three layers. This drawing shows the layers pulled apart so you can picture them more distinctly. They all interconnect and complement one another although each is also believed to contribute specific functions.

The three brain layers can be described as:

- 1st layer or Action Brain (also known as the reptilian brain, sensory-motor brain, or energy brain) – subconscious thought

- 2nd layer or Emotional Brain (sometimes called the pain-pleasure center, limbic system, or mammalian brain) – subconscious thought

- 3rd layer or Thinking Brain (often referred to as the Cerebrum, gray matter, Cortex or Neo-Cortex) – conscious thought

Your Brain and the Senses

Sensory stimuli are believed to enter the brain through nerves in the brain stem, part of the first brain layer. A built-in triage system then sends those stimuli to the appropriate decoding center in the brain. The drawing below shows decoding centers in the two posterior sections of the third brain layer or cerebrum.

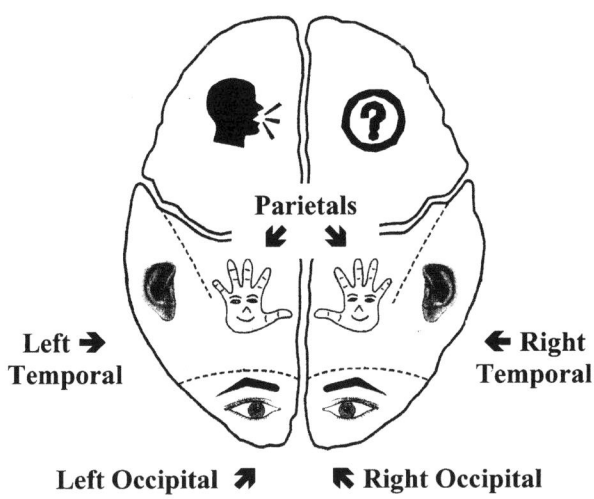

The thinking brain layer (third layer) actually resembles a cap on a toadstool. It is home for conscious thought, although only about 5% of what goes on inside the thinking brain may come to your conscious awareness unless you take steps to increase your awareness.

Your conscious mind is engaged when you are paying attention to something. At the same time your subconscious mind soaks in what you're not consciously paying attention to.

While you are focused on one idea or event, many other processes are occurring simultaneously inside your brain and body—outside your conscious awareness.

For example, a man who is shopping at the hardware store (conscious awareness) could also be psychologically or emotionally influenced by an event that had occurred earlier in the day or by upcoming plans for the evening.

This customer might not consciously notice other shoppers, sale items, loud speaker announcements, or store personnel. But his subconscious mind might. If he stops to talk with a neighbor, his conscious mind moves from shopping to conversing.

To simplify, the conscious mind focuses on the immediate task at hand, while the subconscious mind connects to everything else that's going in the background. Add to this the reality that your subconscious mind is likely the source of all psychosomatic illness. Some researchers estimate that more than 80% of illnesses originate either in the mind or contain a significant mind component.

No wonder Peter McWilliams entitled his book *You Can't Afford the Luxury of a Single Negative Thought.*

So, back to the thinking brain layer. Herein resides the center for your own *innate giftedness*. And that includes sensory preference.

Distribution of Sensory Preference

In adulthood, sensory preference is estimated to occur in the general population in approximately the following distribution:

- Visual – 60%

- Auditory – 20%

- Kinesthetic – 20%

Review the information in the three boxes on the opposite page. In which category do you fall based on your identified sensory preference (refer to Appendix A)?

 **Visual Sensory Preference
60%**

- More males than females

- Ask: who is best at taking data in through sight?

 **Auditory Sensory Preference
20%**

- More females than males

- Ask: Who is best at taking data in through sound?

 **Kinesthetic Sensory Preference
20%**

- Equal numbers of females and males

- Ask: Who is best at taking in data via taste, touch, smell, and body/muscle position?

If You Have Smelled It . . .

All sensory stimuli can be powerful, but odors can trigger memories faster than any other type. Especially odors associated with emotion. For example, your home may include these scents: coffee, chocolate chip cookies, apple pie, your dad's pipe, fresh lilacs in the spring, or vanilla-scented candles. Children from this type of environment will most likely think of home when they come across these scents.

In fact, your nose is just a synapse away from your second brain layer or emotional brain, where incoming sensory information is forwarded to higher centers of association in the third brain layer or thinking brain.

The emotional layer of the brain is thought to generate emotional impulses that impact relationships, bonding, and memory functions.

Think back to a holiday when you gave a gift to someone who did not seem to like it. Perhaps it was not a good match with his or her brain preference. Nevertheless, you felt bad. Or recall a time when you received a gift that was absolutely stellar, one that you had wanted for a long time. If your feelings were hurt or if you felt euphoric, either way you likely stored those events in memory and can recall them.

Emotions are essential for the process of remembering—and sensory memories (especially those involving the sense of smell) are a key component to that. Negative memories can also be triggered by odors: smoke, alcohol, dirty diapers, a musty basement, pollution, disease, sour milk, or a smell associated with an abuser.

And, by the way, decoding scents is part of the kinesthetic sensory system. This means that those with a kinesthetic sensory preference are typically more aware of scents.

Synesthesia – Would you Hear that Coffee!

The term *synesthesia* applies to an interesting neurological phenomenon where the senses are cross-wired (blend, coordinate, and overlap) in an unusual manner. For example, a person with synesthesia may not only *see* or *hear* but also *feel* and *taste* in color, as well.

Approximately one person in 100,000 has profound synesthesia, more heightened in highly creative people and associated with incredible powers of memory.

There is an interesting religious song written and sung by Chris Rice entitled, *Smell the Color Nine*, which ties the idea of finding God to smelling colors. One line states:

*But sometimes finding you is just like
trying to smell the color nine.*

I don't know if you've found God, but I'm quite
sure that some folks have smelled the color nine.

Henri Troyatt, after tasting a coffee ice-cream
soda for the first time was quoted in the *New
York Times* (7-22-92) as saying:

*My taste buds experienced a violent ecstasy.
A whole opera of sensations
rolled off my tongue.*

A Beautiful . . . Hallucination

Hallucinations, described as intense, self-
generated experiences involving one or more of
the senses, have always been a hot topic.
The movie *A Beautiful Mind* (a true story of
Professor John Nash) has gone a long way
toward helping people understand how real these
altered sensory experiences can be.

Hallucinations may sometimes result from the
misrouting of sensory data to the wrong
decoding center. For example, studies have
shown that the voices heard by individuals
diagnosed with schizophrenia are usually their
own. For them, speech generated in one portion
of the brain, is experienced as hearing in another.

On the other hand, hallucinations can also be the result of giftedness. An individual with a photographic memory is thought to be more likely to experience hallucinations.

Children who play with invisible playmates may actually be *seeing* those "friends" as clearly as the rest of us see real people. One mother told of her little boy having created six imaginary brothers, whom he named and talked about regularly. And they could fly. Of course they could fly!

In adulthood, a well-known speaker finally admitted that she had had an imaginary friend all through childhood. Named  *Little John Deerfoot,* this imaginary Native-American boy went everywhere with her, although she was careful not to talk about him to other adults "because I know they would have thought I needed to be locked up in an insane asylum."

She could describe the way *Little John Deerfoot* looked in detail with his hand-crafted leather clothing. She could even describe the sound of his voice as having a "slight French accent."

How silly, you might think. And then again . . . why not? Just because most adults have lost their colorful imaginations doesn't mean children need to. When you study the senses, it all starts to make so much more *sense!*

Knowing Your Sensory Preference

Did you know that your sensory preference impacts the way you learn?

It is generally easier to assimilate information that comes to you in your sensory preference. Conversely, it can be more difficult to absorb information that comes to you in a non-preferred sensory system. Although you usually *can* do so, it can be much more energy-intensive and will be harder to transfer data to your long-term memory banks for later recall.

In other words, if you're Visual, you should *see* what you're trying to learn. If you're Auditory, you need to *hear* the instructions. If you're Kinesthetic, it helps to get your hands involved. (You were fortunate if your teachers consciously incorporated all three sensory systems into their teaching methods.)

Differences in sensory preference underlie many communication problems, situational misunderstandings, and feelings of discomfort. Some Kinesthetic folks like to touch one another and be touched. Others don't. Still others are exceedingly particular about who touches them. Being aware of this *matters.*

Romantic Situations

All three sensory systems (Visual, Auditory, and Kinesthetic) tend to be activated during romantic encounters.

During courtship partners usually talk to each other, listen, and express affection verbally. They take pains to show each other a good time. They may look at each other in that special way and affirm each other's appearance. They touch, hug, kiss . . .

"*Duh,*" you say. Nevertheless, it's easy to perceive why being on the receiving end of this level of multi-sensory stimuli can make one want to spend the rest of his/her life with the nurturer.

Business Environments

All three sensory systems (Visual, Auditory, and Kinesthetic) are often activated during business encounters, as well, especially if the person who is seeking the "contract" understands sensory preference.

For example, contacts often "wine and dine" each other, perhaps take trips to view the property or institution under discussion, and may provide gifts or incentives to spur the negotiations. All things being equal, this type of whole-brain interaction is designed to encourage the other individual(s) to view the proposed partnership, merger, or sale with favor.

Short Half-Life

Unfortunately, these levels of sensory nurturing tend to diminish when the goal of the romantic or business *courtship* has been reached or when the dotted line has been signed (unless you understand this phenomenon and consciously continue the process). Otherwise, each individual again reverts very quickly to a communication style that matches his/her sensory preference.

If the parties' sensory preferences differ, it's not long until the individuals may experience some level of discomfort or discontent, or sense some bewilderment because they "thought he/she was so much like me"—and not understand the reason.

The reason likely is that their sensory preferences differ. Because of this, each eventually begins relating to the other in his/her own sensory preference. And the mismatched sensory stimuli simply don't register in the other person's brain in the same way.

For example:

- A Visual person may dress and groom carefully, give lovely gifts, and take the partner places to see things. But the

Visual person may not talk enough to please the Auditory partner, or may fail to offer sufficient nonsexual touch to help meet the partner's skin-hunger needs.

- An Auditory person may talk of love, but neglect to look at the other person in that special way, may fail to groom carefully, may overlook the planning of outings, or fail to touch appropriately.

- The Kinesthetic partner may be good at touching ("I Wanna Hold Your Haaaaannnnnd"), yet may neglect attentions that would appeal to a Visual (e.g., flowers, movies, beautifully gift-wrapped presents), or to an Auditory person (e.g., verbal communication, books to read, active listening).

Remember Neil Diamond's ballad, *You Don't Bring Me Flowers Any More?* Sung like a true Visual! How about the romantic Kinesthetic line, *You don't have to say you love me, just be close at hand . . .?*

If partners match in their sensory preference, each usually feels nurtured as preferred stimuli register quickly and intensely in his/her brain. But, if the couple's sensory preferences don't match, then sensory preference needs to be understood so partners can affirm each other effectively on a daily basis.

After all, the goal is for each person to feel understood, affirmed, desired, and loved.

An easy way to be sure you cover all the bases is to identify each other's sensory preference and offer specific sensory nurturing every day in your partner's preference. Or, you could just continue to relate to each other in a whole-brained manner. In other words, just do it all. With any luck at all, one type of stimuli will get through to the other person's brain!

Whole Brain with Any Goal

It's far more than this, however. The brain tends to move into automatic whole-brain sensory communication any time it is trying to accomplish a goal. Sometimes that is a romantic goal but often it is a business goal. Some astute individuals have even learned to put sensory preference to their financial advantage. Take George, for example.

George's Story

George is an unbelievably successful real estate agent. When others in sales are moaning and groaning about the flat market or the perceived recession, he regularly manages to connect buyers with sellers.

How?

By understanding the sensory systems, of course, and providing appropriately-matched sensory stimuli.

When homebuyers first enter George's office, he asks them to describe exactly what they want in a home. He carefully watches their body language, listens for key signals through words and phrases, and tries to sense their motivation. Then he matches his sales pitch to their sensory preference. For example:

If buyers appear to be Visual, he may tell them that the house possesses eye appeal and that the windows overlook breath-taking views. He asks them to notice the fine craftsmanship, from the carving on the doors to the trim over the portico.

To tap into the Auditory system, George may talk about the house being soundly constructed, mention the lack of creaks and groans from the floorboards and the excellent insulation to block out undesirable sounds, or call their attention to the rustling of leaves on trees surrounding the property. George would, as appropriate, point out the babbling brook nearby or birds in the bushes, happy sounds of school children from a nearby school, or even the quietude in a country setting.

When George is addressing a primarily Kinesthetic client, he will draw attention to the fine, smooth finishing detail and plush carpets. He may suggest that they touch the wood on the railing or the marble on the countertops. He may point out that the way in which the kitchen window is positioned allows the warmth of the sun to permeate the room. George may talk about the potential for sitting on the wide patio to soak up the perfume from wildflowers growing in the lot next door, or how they will enjoy the raspberries on the bushes near the fence. He may also suggest that the porch would be an ideal location for a swing.

And when George isn't sure which of the three sensory systems might be the most appropriate, he addresses all three. Some of his colleagues poke fun at the "scientific" way in which he approaches sales. They accuse him of using manipulation. George responds that he just understands what works for the brain, and he goes on presenting housing options in a language his customers can understand.

Sensory language.

Effective communication.

It's hard to argue with success.

Victoria's Story

Victoria, a health counselor, uses a similar approach when working with clients who need to regain their health through lifestyle changes. She asks each client to take the *Sensory Preference Assessment* and then utilizes the information to coach each in his/her sensory preference.

For example:

When encouraging smokers to quit, Victoria helps Auditories understand how nice it will be not to hear themselves wheezing and gasping for air as they climb stairs or walk uphill.

Victoria reminds Visuals how great it will be to avoid nicotine stains on their teeth and fingers, burned holes in clothing or blankets, and the "smoke" that floats between conversants and blurs outlines or clouds vision.

Victoria tells Kinesthetics who quit smoking that they can expect to enhance their tasting ability, avoid triggering eye irritation as smoke floats through the air to others, clothing that does not give off the stale smell of tobacco, to say nothing of having nicer breath for sweeter kissing.

Victoria has learned to talk about whatever might get her client's attention, be important to them, and improve their lifestyle and/or lengthen life—in a way that she believes will register most quickly and intensely in the other person's brain.

Clues to Sensory Preference

Okay, by now you may have gained a new perspective about how important knowing one's own sensory preference (as well as that of others) can be in relationships and career settings. It's really not emotionally intelligent to walk up to someone and say, "Will you take this *Sensory Preference Assessment* so I know how to communicate with you?" There are some common clues, however, that can give you some idea of the other person's sensory preference. The lists that follow can prove very helpful.

Visual Sensory Preference – Common Characteristics

 Individuals with a Visual sensory preference may:

- Use visual words and metaphors (e.g., *I see. Picture this. The light just went on. It's crystal clear to me now. She talked until she was blue in the face. Do you see what I mean?*)

- Have a higher-pitched voice

- Tend to speak rapidly

- Breathe shallowly or hold breath at times while thinking

- Draw pictures in the air with arms and hands

- React faster and more intensely to visual stimuli

- Like pets that are interesting to watch (e.g., swimming fish, birds with beautiful plumage, unusually colored or shaped cats or dogs)

- Prefer colorful environments and work spaces

- Want food to look appealing and attractive (e.g., may dislike beets and mashed potatoes blending together on a plate)

- Report having been afraid of the dark or scary movies as a child

- Believe that the way things look is extremely important

- Pick up on the facial expressions of others

- Be hurt or irritated by lack of eye contact and feel affirmed quickly when people look directly into their eyes and smile

- Learn most quickly by seeing how something is done

Auditory Sensory Preference – Common Characteristics

 Individuals with an Auditory sensory preference tend to:

- Use auditory words and metaphors (e.g., *That sounds okay to me. It's clear as a bell. Keep your ear to the ground. That doesn't ring true. Do you hear what I mean?)*

- Exhale deeply and sigh, especially when tired, tense, or stressed

- Cock head to one side when listening carefully or speaking intensely, or may cup or touch ear

- React faster and/or more intensely to auditory stimuli (e.g., sirens, bells, whistles)

- Like pets that make sounds or talk (e.g., parrots, canaries)

- Prefer toys that make sounds

- Want food to sound right (e.g., may like or dislike crunchy sounds)

- Report having been frightened by loud/scary sounds (e.g., thunder, crying, fireworks) as a child

- Pay attention to the sound of clothing (e.g., like/dislike swishing of nylon or clanking of zippers)

- Be sensitive to things they hear in the environment especially discordant sounds (e.g., arguing, yelling, whispering)

- Feel affirmed quickly by positive sounds (e.g., kind words, nature sounds, music, friendly voices)

- Be hurt by lack of positive auditory input (e.g., silent treatment, harsh voices, unpleasant noises)

- Learn most quickly by hearing how something is done through verbal explanations or by written instructions

Kinesthetic Sensory Preference –
Common characteristics

 Individuals with a Kinesthetic sensory preference (taste, odor, touch, position sense) are generally those who:

- Use Kinesthetic words and metaphors (e.g., *That doesn't fit. That doesn't feel right. I've got a gut feeling . . . I'm trying to get in touch with that idea. Let's hammer out a plan. It's as clear as mud. Spare me from the jolting headlines!)*

- Have low-pitched voices

- Tend to breathe deeply and speak slowly

- Prefer to work with their hands

- React faster and/or more intensely to kinesthetic stimuli

- Like pets that are comfortable to touch or hold and are often intuitive with animals

- As a child preferred toys that felt good (e.g., smooth, soft, interesting texture)

- Want food to feel right (e.g., not too hot or cold, not slimy or scratchy) and be tasty (e.g., often lean toward the gourmet)

- May be afraid of pain, physical irritations, or discomfort

- Need their clothing to feel right and not be restrictive, rough, or too hot/cold

  Tip: Avoid purchasing clothes for a Kinesthetic—give them a gift certificate so they can make their own selection (or they may never wear the item you give them because it "doesn't feel right")

- Are highly sensitive to environmental conditions (e.g., temperature, drafts, furniture texture)

- May be hurt by a lack of touch or harsh touch (e.g., spanked, kicked, jerked, hair pulled, held down and tickled)

- Are affirmed quickly when people and/or the environment acknowledges and makes provision for their kinesthesia

- Often learn most quickly by actually touching and doing, hands-on style

Again, you get the idea. Think about your own sensory preference and what "works best for your brain." Now translate that to others.

Career Choices Considering Sensory Preference

Your sensory preference can impact not only the career path toward which you gravitate, but also your situational comfort level while doing key activities. The following are examples of some career paths that might appeal to individuals based on sensory preference (depending, of course, on other factors such as position on the EAI Continuum and brain lead).

Visual Preference

- Airline pilots

- Fire fighters

- Sharp shooters, marksmen

- Entertainers (TV, movies, videos)

- Artisans, designers

- Runway and/or magazine models

- Sign-language translators

- Tasks that require marked visual acuity (e.g., traffic controllers, reading radiographic images)

Auditory Preference

- Musicians
- Psychotherapists
- Counselors
- Speech therapists
- Hosts of talk shows, radio broadcasters
- Public speakers
- Readers
- Telephone communicators
- Foreign language translators
- Voice-over specialists

Kinesthetic Preference

- Athletes
- Dancers
- Some surgeons
- Masseuse/masseur
- Auto mechanics
- Computer programmers, designers
- Artists (especially art forms that use hands in the process)
- Physical and Occupational therapists

Challenges in Today's "Hands-Off" Society . . .

 Every person has skin-hunger needs. In order to thrive, humans require non-sexual, physical-touch affirmation. Unfortunately, many people don't get enough touch validation. And in today's "no-touch" society, individuals with a Kinesthetic sensory preference often suffer the most deprivation. Cultural prohibitions against touching contribute to this. Many people (males especially) are touch-deprived.

Some males are fortunate to have friends or a partner with whom they can exchange touch. Others have pets to handle. Still others try to satisfy their touching needs through sexual activity.

It is critically important for a person with a Kinesthetic preference to take positive steps toward obtaining nonsexual, physical touch. If that person is you, teach your friends to give you nonsexual touch (the type of touch that helps meet skin-hunger needs best).

Allot time to spend with animals that like to be touched, curl up with a soft afghan and a stuffed animal, or soak in the tub amidst your favorite candle fragrances. Make life work for you.

All children require nonsexual touch affirmation just to stay alive. Studies of infants in orphanages showed that without sufficient touch, the babies died. When elderly volunteers were recruited to simply hold the babies an average of fifteen minutes per day, the infants stopped dying. *Amazing.*

Children with a Kinesthetic preference may need affirming touch even more because that type of sensory stimuli registers most quickly and intensely in their brains. Children who do not get their touch needs met appropriately may fail to thrive or learn, may be more vulnerable to inappropriate touch (e.g., physical or sexual abuse), or may be at a higher risk for unwed pregnancies.

All human beings require nonsexual touch affirmation, although individuals with a Kinesthetic preference often present a challenging paradox. Although they generally relate to the world through touch, taste, smell, position/posture, and sensitivity to the environment, they can also be extremely discriminating about who touches them. Avoid potentially bruising Kinesthetics through unwelcome, intrusive, or insensitive touch.

Again, if this is you, learn to communicate kindly and firmly the type of touch you desire or are willing to tolerate. It's your brain's sensory preference, and you understand it best.

Everyone Likes to Feel Real

 One evening, a family decided to go out for dinner at their favorite restaurant. They were shown to a table that overlooked the bay, and within minutes the waitress arrived to take their order. She began with the father and asked each member in turn what he or she wanted. Finally reaching the youngest family member, the waitress asked, "And what would you like to eat, young lady?"

"A burger and fries," the little girl answered politely.

"Bring her lasagna," said the mother.

"And what would you like to drink?" the waitress continued.

"Sprite, please," the child replied.

"Bring her lasagna and milk," the mother said firmly. The waitress looked from the mother to the little girl, back to the mother, and then wrote down the order.

In due time, the food arrived. To the delight of the wee customer (and the consternation of her mother!), the waitress placed a burger, fries, and Sprite in front of the little girl.

The child looked at her plate. Eyes glowing with excitement, she fairly shouted in a voice that carried to the far corners of the restaurant, "Mommy, Mommy! That lady thinks I'm real!"

Increase Your Awareness

Ask yourself a few questions:

- Are you naturally aware of sensory preference?

- Do you know your own sensory preference?

- Have you learned to be aware of clues that suggest the sensory preference of others?

- Do you use the sensory systems by design to help people around you feel *real*?

- When you don't know someone's sensory preference do you consciously utilize all three sensory systems to increase the odds that you will better connect with that person's brain?

Paying attention to the sensory systems and sensory preference is critically important. Do something often for others (e.g., partner, children, friends, or co-workers) in their sensory preference. Then, sit back and watch your relationships improve.

Another growth step involves learning to recognize and graciously accept nurturing from others even when it doesn't come in your preferred style—but in theirs. If you develop this skill you are a most wise individual. Others may try to affirm you by using activities or strategies that match *their* sensory preference (not yours).

Failing to recognize, acknowledge, or accept their affirmation just because it didn't come to you in your sensory preference can represent a missed opportunity.

Avoid missing out on validation and affirmation simply because it isn't packaged the way you prefer. But there are also ways to let others know your sensory preference, since they obviously want to please you. Make sensory preference part of your everyday language.

For example:

- You are Auditory and receive a DVD from someone who is a Visual. You might say, "Thank you for thinking of me. I notice the music on this DVD was composed by *so-and-so*. Since I am an Auditory I will probably especially enjoy the music as I watch this DVD."

- You are Visual and you are given some fragrant soap by a Kinesthetic. You might say, "I appreciate this gift and will hone my Kinesthesia while I use it. Because my primary sensory preference is Visual, the color of this bar really appeals to me."

- You are Kinesthetic and receive a cookbook. You might say, "Did you know I am a Kinesthetic and really enjoy scents and tastes? It will be fun to try some of these recipes!"

Talk the language! This validates their gifts even as you recognize and appreciate their efforts—and enhances their understanding of your sensory preference. You get the idea.

Tips for Enhancing Your Sensory Skills

Communication and behaviors that acknowledge and nurture sensory preference are learned. Here are some tips to consider:

- **Knowledge** - Identify your own sensory preference and then be alert to situations that could be enhanced through applying what you know.

- **Choice** - Choose to practice whole-brained sensory behaviors whenever possible (e.g., when greeting others look them in the eye, shake hands, and say something).

- **Competency** - Develop skills in all three sensory systems. That way you will be ready for almost any type of situation.

- **Practice** - Competency is honed by thoughtful practice. Consistent, thoughtful practice on a daily basis.

- **Creativity** - Be innovative in using the sensory systems. Try something new when communicating with others. Avoid doing the same thing over and over again, or believing that simply because something worked once it will work all the time.

- **Implementation** - Communicate with others in their sensory preference. Do something every day for your close friends/family members in their sensory preference. The sensory stimuli will register quickly and more intensely in their brains, helping them to feel comfortable, cared about, and affirmed.

The bottom line? When unsure of someone's sensory preference, use all three!

Yep, Seeing is Believing

Is it really?

The myth has always been that *seeing* is believing. It may be for Visuals. But the fact is this: no, sometimes believing comes through hearing certain *sounds* or receiving specific types of *touch, tastes,* or *scents.*

In Shel Silverstein's popular poetry book *Where the Sidewalk Ends,* readers are gently reminded about the impact of sharing love. The picture shows a forlorn little person holding a poster on which is written the letter "V."

The verse reads:

> *Ricky was "L," but he's home with the flu.*
> *Lizzie, "O," had some homework to do.*
> *Mitchell, "E," prob'ly got lost on the way.*
> *So I'm all the love that could make it today.*

If no one else is around to do it, if no one else is around who understands it, the job (or the joy) could just become yours.

Using sensory stimuli by design (rather than by default) could make a positive difference in someone's life. Maybe even in your own.

Point To Ponder

*If I read a book and it makes my body so cold
no fire can warm me, I know that is poetry.
If I feel physically as if the top of my head were
taken off, I know that is poetry.
These are the only ways I know it.
Is there any other way?*

—Emily Dickinson

Chapter Seven

Up the Down Escalator—Ignoring your bent can get you nowhere fast!

Ignoring who you truly, authentically are can literally be killing you . . . Forcing yourself to be someone you are not, or stuffing down who you really are, is incredibly taxing . . . It will tax you so much that it will shorten your life by years and years.

Philip C. McGraw, *Self Matters*

A familiar slogan, probably intended to be a word of encouragement, says: "Do it anyway. It builds character."

Is this saying another of Grandpa's truisms—or merely a part of the great American myth? Either way, current brain research doesn't appear to agree. And as Dr. Phil's quote above states, forcing yourself to "do it anyway" could even shorten your life.

Doing things you don't like (and doing them often) doesn't necessarily build character. More likely such activities will create anxiety, bitterness, and frustration or, as we've been saying, *brain drain*. Who knew?

However, people who have absorbed such beliefs and expectations often struggle their entire lives trying to develop skills in areas that are exceedingly difficult, if not downright exhausting—kind of like trying to ascend an escalator that is on its way down. Not your best choice if you want to live a long life that's healthy, happy, and successful.

Competencies

Competencies are simply skills that have been honed through practice.

You can develop competencies in areas of innate preference as well as non-preference. When the skills you develop match your innate preference, you're usually able to achieve high levels of competency. That means you become better at performing those skills than many others.

For example:

- Who should invest in expensive voice lessons? Someone who can't hold a tune or someone with a natural singing ability?

- Who should hire an experienced tennis coach? Someone who has never held a racket or someone who has already shown him/herself to be proficient in the game?

- Who should consider a career in nursing? Someone who has always exhibited empathy in the presence of illness or injury or someone who runs the other way at the sight of blood?

Hone the skills you are already good at and that your brain handles energy-efficiently—and see how far you can go. (Unless you're just game for trying something new on a temporary basis.)

 Here's an example many have tried. Place a pen or pencil in your favored writing hand and sign your name. You are now exhibiting a developed competency in an area of preference. Handedness. Now put the pen or pencil in your non-favored writing hand and sign your name. Observe differences in ease of

writing, legibility, and amounts of energy expended.

When you write with your non-preferred hand, the activity will generally require a higher expenditure of energy and result in a lower level of comfort. You might improve your writing by that non-preferred hand through practice, but the energy expenditure will still be higher than when writing with your preferred hand.

Here's another example. Fold your hands, fingers interlocking, in your preferred style. You probably do this so automatically that you followed this direction without giving it much thought. Look at your folded hands. Which thumb is on top—right or left? How comfortable do your hands feel?

Now refold your hands, interlocking your fingers so that the opposite thumb is on top. Now how comfortable do your hands feel? (You may want to do a similar exercise by folding your arms first one way and then the opposite way.)

This exercise demonstrates the phenomenon known as *adaption*. You can fold your hands the opposite way, but it's unlikely that it will ever feel as comfortable as your preferred folding style. Even though you can't observe it as easily as the hand-folding exercise, a similar phenomenon happens inside your brain when you utilize non-preferred functions.

Activities that involve adaption are never quite as comfortable as those that match your brain lead—and always take more energy.

Building Competencies

You may have deliberately chosen to develop skills throughout your thinking brain, even while deliberately striving for a majority match between your activities and brain preferences. (Or maybe you'll choose to do so now.) If that's the case, here are samplings of competency-building activities, separated according to the four divisions of the third brain layer or thinking brain. (Keep in mind there could be some overlap.)

Review the lists on the following page. You may recognize that several activities (or other similar activities) probably energize you. Others don't and you would probably choose to avoid them, even for money!

This can help to give you an idea which cerebral division contains your brain's *bent*. Treat yourself to that activity today. (After all, tomorrow you may have to adapt.)

As Socrates put it:

> *The surest way to live with honor*
> *in the world is to be in reality what we*
> *would appear to be.*

Left Frontal Lobe

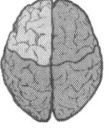

- Join a debate club
- Give a speech in public
- Read information and write a summary or abstract
- Participate in a research project

Right Frontal Lobe

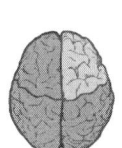

- Write poems and stories
- Learn to meditate
- Compose and/or arrange music
- Draw, paint, sculpt, carve, design, assemble 3-D puzzles, travel

Left Posterior Lobes

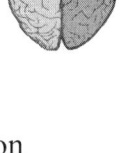

- Make and follow lists
- Balance the checkbook
- Join a club or team
- Learn to sight-read music
- Read and outline information

Right Posterior Lobes

- Join a choir
- Take a drama class
- Play games for fun
- Participate in peer counseling
- Play an instrument by ear

Adaption Relates to What?

The concept of adaption relates to an ability to change in order to be able to fit into a new or specified situation. In brain-function terminology, it refers to the development and use of competencies or skills that do not match one's areas of preference.

The concept of adaption can apply to any area of brain function (e.g., spending large amounts of time functioning at a non-preferred position on the Gender Continuum, or the EAI Continuum, or repressing your preferred sensory system). And, of course, it plays a huge role if you fail to identify and utilize your brain's *bent.*

All human beings adapt from time to time because it offers them additional options—and that's good. How limited life would be if people tried to function only from a position of innate preference 100% of the time.

An individual whose brain bent favors the right frontal lobe may be quite entrepreneurial or artistically creative. However, that same individual also might want the option to be able to balance a checkbook (left posterior lobes), connect with friends and family (right posterior lobes), and analyze key reports or make decisions about financial investment (left frontal lobe). Those choices represent helpful and temporary adaption.

The UPs and DOWNs of Adaption

Adaption can actually increase your options. Your overall potential for success increases when you have developed skills throughout your brain. **That's the up side**.

However, spending the majority of your time performing activities that are non-preferred can be exhausting. **That's the down side.**

Mel Levine, author of *A Mind at a Time*, put it like this:

> *Nothing is as stressful as trying to be a different person from who you are.*

Remember: there is a huge difference between what you have learned to do well and what your brain does energy-efficiently.

Sarah's Story

Sarah sat slumped in the chair, head in her hands. "I'm so exhausted I can't put one foot in front of the other!" she moaned. Sarah had worked in the family-owned business for eighteen years. The detail that was required to offer a reliable service to customers drained her energy. Not only was she perpetually tired, some rather serious health problems had cropped up.

When the doctor suggested that Sarah apply the energy-evaluation process to her activities both at home and at work, she was amazed at what she uncovered (refer to Appendix B). Together they worked out a plan of action, beginning with a schedule of after-work activities that were easier and more energy-efficient for Sarah's brain.

 Often, by the end of her chosen activity (e.g., art class at a local Community College or singing alto with the community choir), Sarah felt as if she had more energy than when she had started. And she was also sleeping better.

With some measure of trepidation (a few family members were quite verbal about Sarah's need to avoid being selfish and lazy), she hired a part-time housekeeper. This freed up time to engage in activities that she truly enjoyed and decreased some of the energy drain.

Adaption Caveats

Sarah did not quit her job: she just tweaked her lifestyle to include activities that worked for her brain preference. Adaption represents the quintessential "different strokes for different folks" philosophy.

Note these three caveats:

- An activity that constitutes adaption in one person can represent giftedness in another

- An activity that energizes one person can exhaust another

- An activity that one individual can ace at high levels of competence may be virtually impossible for another

Why are these truisms so critically important to understand? Because even within one's own family such differences are often found. They need to be recognized and celebrated.

For some, learning to balance their checkbook and doing it every month could be fun. For another, that might be an exhausting but worthwhile adaption. However, in the second case, the individual probably would be well advised to avoid becoming an accountant, bookkeeper, or CPA for eight or ten hours a day.

One individual might adapt by offering a listening ear as a peer counselor for a few hours a month. But working full time as a counselor would likely represent undesirable adaption, which could lead to burnout and/or mid-life crisis.

Writing a short article for the newspaper might help a person build desirable skills. Expecting to earn his or her living as a top-paid writer might be an entirely different matter.

 The key to success is to use adaption for short periods of time ("temporary adaption") rather than long periods ("prolonged adaption"). Stay attuned to the amount of brain energy required.

Adaption Costs

In life you usually give up something to get something. As beneficial as temporary adaption can be, there *is* a cost. Human beings pay for adaption in some way or another—mostly in life energy. Benziger, creator of the Benziger Thinking Styles Assessment or BTSA that includes information on one's risk for adaption, summarizes the cost of adaption as follows:

- The immediate results tend to be that second for second the brain works much harder (e.g., increased need for oxygen, glucose, and other nutrients)

- The short-term results tend to be an increase in irritability, headaches, and difficulty in mastering new tasks

- The long-term results tend to include the potential for exhaustion, depression, lack of joy, a homeostatic imbalance involving oxygen and glucose, premature aging of the brain, and a vulnerability to illness

Triggers for Prolonged Adaption

People adapt for a variety of reasons. Many different situations can push you toward prolonged adaption. Examples include:

- A mismatch between your brain's *bent* and societal expectations for your gender (e.g., a female who is gifted in auto mechanics or research, a male who is gifted in home decorating or cooking)

- A mismatch between your innate giftedness and expected or imposed guidelines for behaviors (e.g., your religion discourages dancing or acting; a teacher demeans your musical or artistic talent, your parents insist on you pursuing a specific career)

- Your position in the sibling line-up (e.g., an oldest or only son is expected to take over the family farm or go into a family-owned business regardless of personal desire or aptitude)

- Being rewarded for adaptive behaviors or shamed for your innate giftedness (e.g., "You're smart enough to be a doctor. Forget teaching." Or "You're not smart enough to be a doctor. Be a nurse instead." Or "No son of mine is going to be a namby-pamby artist." Or "We want you to follow a career in _____ just like members of this family have always done.")

- Living in an environment that involves mental, emotional, sexual, physical, or spiritual abuse (e.g., you cope by becoming involved in an addictive behavior, you conform to expectations regardless of how much energy it requires and move toward exhaustion, you become more and more angry or more and more depressed and become testy with others or develop a personal illness or both)

- Demands of a crisis situation or a lack of opportunity for activities that match your innate giftedness (e.g., you are gifted in creative writing but have no time to spend on it, having been left to care for the family; you have musical talent but there is no money for lessons or instruments; your choice of a profession is not encouraged or the education is unavailable in your area)

- Wanting to copy and be like a loved family member or disowning characteristics of a disliked member (e.g., your professor-father abandons the family and, although you sense a calling to be a teacher, you don't want to be like him; your favorite aunt is a nurse and you want to be just like her, even though many of her nursing activities are energy-intensive for your brain)

- A search for personal identity (e.g., you attempt to differentiate from your identical twin; you try to excel in activities that are rewarded in your family, even though they don't match your innate preferences; you attempt to succeed by excelling in something that is different from what other family members do; you try to live up to the reputation set by an older sibling)

The Goal: Living Authentically

Being real and living authentically involves knowing your innate preferences (your brain's energy advantage and what it does most easily), and making conscious choices related to the amount of time you spend adapting (performing activities that require much higher expenditures of energy second for second).

Have you *ever* lived authentically? Thinking about tomorrow, will the majority of your activities match your innate preferences?

If your answers are *yes* and *yes,* you likely know what it feels like to be "real." You probably know how to manage your energy expenditures efficiently. If the answers are *no* and *no,* this may be new territory for you. You will likely need to learn how your brain feels when it is purring along in an energy-efficient manner.

Tom's Story

From the time he was a little boy visiting his uncle's ranch, Tom had been fascinated by big machines. No surprise that he became a heavy equipment operator. Reluctantly, due to family pressure, he returned to school. Upon graduation he took over managing the books in his father's prestigious law office.

As time went by, however, Tom's health began to deteriorate and signs of depression surfaced.  Medication helped, but didn't cure his fatigue and boredom. His uncle, concerned about his favorite nephew, invited Tom to spend a couple weeks on the ranch. By the time he returned home, Tom had decided to resign his job with the law firm and return to his first love—operating heavy equipment.

Tom's wife tells the story this way: "When Tom bounded up the steps with energy he hadn't shown for years, I knew I had my husband back."

Symptoms of Over-Adaption

Why is it so important to identify and resolve prolonged adaption?

The short answer is that the cost of prolonged adaption is high. It involves expending life energy that is, consequently, unavailable for other endeavors and that, over time, depletes one's energy banks too quickly.

The long answer is more involved. In the long term, prolonged adaption, with its increased drain on vital energy, can lead to a variety of challenges, which can include the following:

- Progressive procrastination
- Fatigue moving toward exhaustion
- Risk of illness
- Frustration
- Risk of burnout and/or midlife crisis
- Falling levels of self-esteem
- Decreased emotional tone
- Interference with ability to concentrate
- Failure to thrive in life
- Diminished success overall

In other words, adaption is a form of stress. It can become a major stressor when it's excessive or prolonged. If you spend years living at high levels of adaption, living an inauthentic life, the outcome of the stress can eventually show itself in all the ways just listed, and more.

Prolonged Adaption Stress Syndrome

In her work, Taylor observed anecdotally that individuals who were struggling to accomplish activities that were energy-exhausting for their brain, often exhibited a cluster of specific symptoms. The longer and more frequently they had been doing this (e.g., prolonged adaption), the more symptoms or higher severity of symptoms they tended to exhibit.

Other individuals exhibited some (but not all) of the cluster of syndromes and often reported that some portions of their lives were working quite well, while others were not. When they were engaged in activities that matched what their brains did energy-efficiently they felt good, but when the opposite occurred, they felt drained.

Eight specific symptoms were eventually identified as comprising the cluster. Taylor assigned the label Prolonged Adaption Stress Syndrome or PASS for short, to this cluster.

- **Fatigue**

  This makes sense, especially when the brain must work significantly harder when adapting. The risk here is self-medicating with anything that will alter brain chemistry and make the person feel better and less exhausted—however temporary (e.g., food, beverages, drugs, addictive behaviors).

- **Hypervigilance**

  This can become a safety mechanism for the brain. It tends to go on "protective alertness" in response to the mismatch between who it is innately and the energy-exhausting activities it is trying to complete.

- **Immune System Suppression**

  Over time, suppression of immune system function can show itself in slowed rates of healing and/or an increased susceptibility to illness (e.g., cold or flu, autoimmune diseases, cancer). The brain and immune system are in constant communication. According to Dr. Paris Kidd, a biomedical nutritionist, if people took proper care of their immune system, the average life span could reach well over 100 years—at high levels of mental and physical functioning.

- **Interference with Frontal Lobe Functions**

  The stress of adaption, which can alter neurochemicals throughout the brain, can be especially deleterious when it occurs in the frontal and pre-frontal lobes (the "executive" portions of the third brain layer). This may be reflected in a decrease in artistic and creative endeavors, a reduced ability to brainstorm options, interference with an ability to make logical/rational decisions, and in slowed speed of thinking. When you say, "I just can't think," you are probably right on the money. Something isn't working optimally in your brain.

Note: An alteration in brain chemistry may also impact one's management of willpower, the development and use of conscience, and one's behavioral choices. This is an attention-getting concept, especially when some behaviors can impact the next generation. Some researchers have even suggested that humans may be unable to access free will or be truly intimate with another (intellectually, emotionally, physically, sexually, or spiritually) unless they are being authentically "real."

- **Memory Problems**

  Cortisol, a body substance that is released under stress, can interfere with the function of memory in a variety of ways, including actually killing brain cells. For more information on this topic, refer to Dr. Robert Sapolsky's book, *Why Zebras Don't Get Ulcers.*

- **Discouragement/Depression**

  Some estimates indicate that 20 million people in the United States are depressed at any given time, with 15% of those likely being suicidal. Prolonged adaption may contribute to such statistics because of the profound energy drain it can cause over time.

- **Self-Esteem Problems**

  This isn't hard to imagine. You don't feel successful in life, you have many of the other listed symptoms, and you feel "trapped." No wonder you question your self-worth. A diary by Christopher Isherwood called *Goodbye to Berlin* opens this way: "I am a camera with its shutter open, quite passive, recording, not thinking." What a monotonous, unrewarding, and weary way to move through life.

Adaption's Impact on Neurons

As mentioned earlier, neurons are specialized cells that have a unique ability to transfer information from one to another. Unfortunately, neurons can be negatively impacted by everything from lack of sleep to inadequate diet or chronic stress.

Brent Hafen in his book *Mind/Body Health* reported that brain cells are destroyed by stress, especially in the hippocampus (involved with learning and memory).

It's worth repeating:

Chronic stress from failure to live authentically
can shorten your potential longevity
by a decade or more.

Not a good choice, in most people's book!
Therefore, how certain activities adversely
impact neurons over time should be high on a
person's list of "Things Worth Investigating."

Stress of Adaption

Some of the ways in which the stress of
prolonged adaption can eventually show itself
(outlined above) are similar to factors (listed
below) that can impact neurons in a negative
way:

- Chronic disease (especially heart disease)
- Unresolved grief over personal loss
- Alcohol (immoderate use)
- A sedentary lifestyle
- Lack of stimulation
- Malnutrition
- Some drugs/medications
- Depression
- A low educational level and an absence
  of curiosity or desire to learn

Aging and Adaption

Avoiding and/or resolving prolonged adaption can help you go lightly into old age. This means that in and of itself, aging (in the absence of prolonged adaption) does not need to have a huge negative impact on the deterioration of brain function.

Many individuals have found their path, followed their innate brain preferences, and continued to make valuable contributions to the world as senior citizens. Think of these:

- Franz Joseph Haydn wrote the *Creation* at age 67

- Richard Wagner composed the opera *Parsifal* at age 69

- Katherine Hepburn was still acting in movie roles in her 70s

- Merce Cunningham was still dancing in his 70s

- Giuseppi Verdi wrote the opera *Falstaff* at age 80

- Grandma Moses started a new career in painting in her 70s

- Arthur Fiedler was conducting music until his death at age 88

- Martha Graham was still choreographing in her 90s

- Photographer Imogen Cunningham was still taking pictures in her 90s

None of them spring chickens. That's good news. Actually, that's great news! And even better news would be for you to follow suit.

Leaving a Legacy—The Bigger Picture

One gift that adults can pass along to the next generation is to role model functionality. In fact, it may be the greatest gift one can bequeath, since children tend to copy what is modeled to them.

Stories abound of elderly individuals who have said, "If I only had it to do over again . . . " Or, "If only I could go back for just one day and undo that mistake."

Unfortunately, no one can do it over again. Fortunately, it is possible to learn from the mistakes of others and from emerging research. Prevention beats attempts at cure every time!

Spielberg's Story

Steven Spielberg's mother encouraged her son's passion for filmmaking. Once she intentionally cooked a gallon of cherries jubilee (so the story goes) until it exploded in a pressure cooker. Steven wanted to film the gooey mess in the kitchen. "We never had a chance to say no. Steven didn't understand that word!" his mother has been quoted as saying.

Children need to learn that the English language contains the powerful two-letter word *no*. However, Spielberg's mother obviously made judicious decisions about when to use that word and when not to. If she had not encouraged her son to follow his own *bent*—even helping him to do—the world might not have *E.T.* or *Schindler's List*.

Sam Gilliam, addressing the 4MAT Renewal Conference in 1996, said:

> *Creative energy not allowed to develop will express itself in power gone bad.*
> *Creative power gone bad is evil.*

Evaluating Your Own Shortsightedness

Is there anyone anywhere in America who hasn't read the book entitled *Tuesdays with Morrie?* On the national bestseller list for years, it tells the story of how journalist Mitch Albom spent Tuesdays with his former professor Morrie Schwartz—to listen and learn. As Morrie lay dying of Lou Gehrig's disease, he mentored his young friend (and readers) with wisdom about life, love, and death. And *dancing.*

On the eleventh Tuesday, the topic was "our culture." The aged professor speaks:

> *Look, no matter where you live, the biggest defect we human beings have is our shortsightedness. We don't see what we could be. We should be looking at our potential, stretching ourselves into everything we can become.*

Morrie had it right! One good reason to avoid prolonged adaption is to set a stellar example for others to follow, both young and old.

Finding your way through life can literally be a challenge—even a mess. And sometimes a bit like negotiating a mine field. That's okay. If you're open to it, you can learn more from your mistakes than you ever can from your successes.

Be open to also learning from the mistakes of others. Eleanor Roosevelt encouraged people to do this, saying,

> *You can't live long enough to make all of them yourself!*

A Step at a Time

If you tap into the courage needed to actually be who you were meant to be, that could very well be the spark that empowers others to do the same. Do it one step at a time. But do it. Each experience can build on the previous one.

Mark Twain said it this way,

A person who has had a bull by the tail once, has learned 60 or 70 times as much as a person who hasn't.

That's the inestimable value of experience. Of course it will take some practice, especially if you've played unhelpful games for a long time, or have spent years living in prolonged adaption.

But there are ways to manage adaption. Strategies to help you tweak your journey towards thriving.

Here are four to consider:

- **Mentoring**

   Find a mentor to help you develop skills in your areas of innate giftedness, or outside your innate preferences, if your life needs those at the present time

166

- **Collaborating**

  Work with others who have different innate preferences. Listen and learn from their giftedness

- **Sandwiching**

  Insert non-preferred activities between those that your brain relates to easily. Alternate the activities you like to do with those that are less enjoyable and more energy-draining

- **Trading**

  Trade with others—each contributing what his/her brain prefers to do. You cut her hair, she balances your checkbook. You do the research, he writes the report. The potential is limitless

Randy's Story

When Randy was eighteen and one week away from high school graduation, a prominent physician and close family friend invited him to lunch. During the conversation, the doctor made Randy an astounding offer.

"Randy," the doctor said, "I want to offer you a deal. I've been an orthopedic surgeon in this town for over thirty years.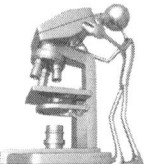

As you know, I've built up a big practice. None of my children were interested in pursuing medicine. I'll pay your way through medical school to become a surgeon, if you'll join my practice and take over when I retire."

Whew! Randy stopped home after the lunch appointment and told his family the story. Then he just sort of laughed, shrugged, and left the room. His mother ran after him, desperate, calling, "Wait, Randy! So, what did you say?"

"Mom," he retorted patiently. "You know I'm not cut out to be a doctor. I don't feel the least called into medicine. Besides, I don't like blood!"

His mother could only whisper, "Well, did you tell him about your sister? She loves blood . . ."

Not too many young adults would turn down such a "gift" worth several hundred thousand dollars in education, to say nothing of a ready-made future in the field of medicine.

Initially, Randy's family thought he was flaming crazy. But in retrospect, after some reflection, his mother knew in her heart that while Randy could have made it through medical school (blood or not), he would have been absolutely miserable in such a career.

Somehow Randy's brain told him what was right for his future—*and he had paid attention!*

A Price Versus Priceless!

Yes, there is a price to pay for prolonged adaption. It differs for different individuals, of course. Nevertheless, resolving prolonged adaption has the potential to result in a positive impact on your health, your happiness, your energy, your relationships, your career, and your overall success in life.

 Metaphorically, think of this process (of matching 51% of your life's activities with your brain's energy advantage) as cutting the cost of prolonged adaption in half.

If you've never lived your innate giftedness, it will be a new journey. Some might even say *priceless.* If you have, but got caught in the trap of prolonged adaption, it's time to return *home*—to your brain's innate giftedness.

Your brain can hardly wait!

Point To Ponder

The concept of downshifting appears to fit with both what is now known about the triune nature of the human brain, and what can continually be seen happening in instructional settings and in daily living. Learning failure results when threat shuts down the brain. The neocortex functions fully only when one feels secure.

—Leslie A. Hart in
Human Brain and Human Learning

Chapter Eight

Downshifting—
Brain *Dent* Alert

Please! That is not your mind speaking, it's the foam of churned feelings and has no meaning.

Nero Wolfe, speaking to his daughter in
Fer-de-Lance, by Rex Stout

'Tis such a pity that today's teenagers can't experience the *thrill* of learning how to drive a manual stick shift—moving forward without jerking, changing gears without squealing, chugging up a steep hill because you forgot to downshift, killing the engine when the light turns green, and learning *how* and *when* to squeal your tires. Such skills kept parents in the passenger seats longer, tensions high.

That was also the era when driving, talking on a cell phone, and drinking coffee simultaneously would be a Herculean challenge—since your right hand had full-time *duty* on the gear shift. (Remember *four-on-the-floor*?)

171

Of course, today's automatic transmissions adjust to varying driving conditions, too (*automatically*), but it's not nearly as exciting, challenging—or as much fun.

And it's an equal shame that the last several generations grew up not learning much about their brains. Many of my experienced teacher-friends went all through undergrad and grad school without ever even hearing the word "brain" once in their college or university classes. They would have so grasped the phenomenon of how brains can "downshift" and "upshift."

(You younger readers will have to just think: on your Schwinn bike, 45 degree hill, wind against you, pedaling furiously, and thankful for ten gears!)

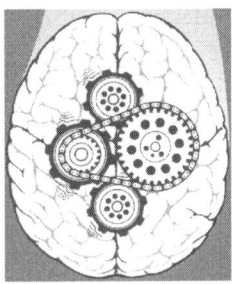 Metaphorically, the three brain layers—action, emotional, thinking—can be compared to gears in a vehicle with an automatic transmission. When you're engaged in activities that honor your brain's *bent*, think of yourself as cruising along in third gear. But if you encounter something fearful, uncomfortable, traumatic, or stressful, your brain's tendency will be to downshift. Automatically.

It's that simple—and that complicated. You've probably experienced this scenario or one similar to it. You and a friend are having a deep conversation in the car. Suddenly, in your rearview mirror, you notice a patrol car, lights flashing. Your brain downshifts instantly.

Your friend, continuing the conversation, says, "So, what do you think about that idea?" Your brain having downshifted, you have no idea about that *idea* or even what you were just talking about! When you pull off the road and the officer shows up at your car door, you'll be lucky to remember your *name*.

 That's downshifting. An unexpected jerk, a sudden process of slowing down or halting cognitive abilities. A focusing of attention and energy toward one of the two lower layers as the brain perceives a lack of safety. You may even feel a sense of helplessness or fatigue. When survival matters, downshifting is both helpful—and unhelpful.

That's why this book must include a chapter on *downshifting*, a natural brain phenomenon, working up the gears, so to speak. Some researchers actually use the term *downshifting* because most people find it quite easy to understand the concept using this metaphor. Some researchers (e.g., Sylwester and others), however, use the terms *reflective* and *reflexive*.

Layers and Gears

Back to the three brain layers being metaphorically analogous to gears in a vehicle that has an automatic transmission: the diagram below portrays one way of picturing this correlation.

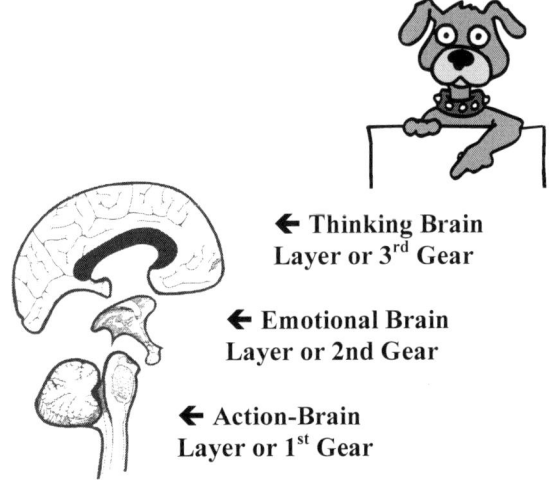

← **Thinking Brain Layer or 3rd Gear**

← **Emotional Brain Layer or 2nd Gear**

← **Action-Brain Layer or 1st Gear**

Action Brain Layer (1st Gear)

The action brain is also referred to as the Sensory/Motor Brain, Reptilian Brain, Energy Brain, or the "id." It consists of the brain stem, portions of the spinal cord, and the cerebellum.

The action brain tends to dominate when threat is perceived, when safety and survival become top priorities. It provides an awareness of your outer sensory world and carries the message "I need to look out for me."

It perceives primarily the present tense and is usually the last portion of the brain to die.

Examples of functions of the action brain:

- Initiates fast protective reflexes and survival strategies in a perceived crisis situation

- Houses automatic and/or ritualistic behaviors

- Can change behavior, much like a chameleon changes color, depending on what it perceives is required or would be safer in a specific environment

- Reacts instinctually to stressors (e.g., fight/flight, tend/befriend, conserve/withdraw) although it tends to resist change

- Alerts the thinking layer in emergency situations to mobile systems for defense

- Maintains functions critical to life (e.g., food and waste disposal, security, comfort)

- Houses the Reticular Activating System (RAS) that influences one's position on the EAI Continuum (Refer to Chapter Five)

- Learns and performs rapid, highly skilled movements (e.g., swimming, running, speaking, keyboard playing)

- Compares command signals (intentions for movement) with sensory information (actual performance) and sends out corrective signals

If you're walking down the street and a humungous dog leaps over the fence and prepares to attack you, your leg might instinctively swing out to kick it away. That's your action brain engaged in a nearly instantaneous "reflexive" behavior. With no time to map out a flowchart of possible options to keep from getting bitten, your action brain triggers a defensive reaction. Your foot flies out. After all, better to kick the dog than have the dog take a bite out of you!

Emotional Brain Layer (2nd Gear)

The emotional brain has also been referred to as the Mammalian Brain, Relational Brain, Limbic Brain, and the Pain/Pleasure Center. It consists of a rim of cerebral cortex on the medial surface of each hemisphere and includes a collection of relatively small brain organs, including the amygdala, the mammillary bodies, the cingulated gyrus (above the corpus callosum), the parahippocampal gyrus (in the temporal lobe below), and the hippocampus.

Even though you may not be familiar with any of those anatomical labels, you *are* well acquainted with the word *emotion.* Emotion, the foundation for all relationships, is sometimes thought of as the "ego." It senses "You are here" and "I am here too." This layer is also believed to be involved with all addictive behaviors.

Examples of functions contributed by the emotional brain:  **←2nd**

- Plays a role in a range of emotions, with many direct connections to the right hemisphere of the thinking layer (but sparse connections to the left hemisphere)

- Generates emotional impulses and plays a role in the processing/monitoring of emotion, essential for the process of remembering

- Appears to be involved with managing associations (building blocks of memory), helps transfer information from short-term to long-term memory

- Searches the brain to collect pieces of information needed in order to recall a memory

- Processes the senses of smell directly— one synapse away from the nose

- Processes information 80,000 times faster than the thinking brain

- Serves as the connection between the thinking brain and the outside world

- Maintains a balance between thinking layer and action layer (i.e., keeps the action layer from totally dominating the thinking layer)

- Translates information from the thinking layer into a language that can be read by the action brain

- Controls the immune system, so it should be no surprise that emotions have a profound effect on the functioning of the immune system

- Is the brain region likely to be the most sensitive to stressors; tends to rev up (i.e., run "hotter," associated with a negative/depressive state of mind) in response to trauma

Another Canine Story

Let's say you pass a pet store and see a sad puppy lying in the window next to a *FOR SALE* sign. He reminds you of a dog you had as a child—a dog you slept with and took to the park. Without thinking about the time and cost of caring for a pet (especially an untrained puppy!) or whether your "roommate" even wants a dog, you walk into the store and walk out with the puppy. Again, the thinking layer of your brain took a back seat to your emotional brain.

178

And the puppy couldn't be happier. (Your roommate may be a different story.)

Thinking Brain Layer (3rd Gear)

The thinking brain is also known by other names: Cognitive Brain, Cerebrum, Gray Matter, Cortex, or Neo-Cortex. Consisting of two cerebral hemispheres, it accounts for most of the tissue (e.g., perhaps 80%) housed inside the bony skull.

This third layer registers awareness of present, past, and future tenses, along with perceiving both positives and negatives. It provides functions related to consciousness (e.g., knowing what you're doing, making choices). It can be compared to the "super-ego" and is able to think of the good of others.

The thinking brain contributes executive aspects of thought (e.g., planning, goal-setting, paying attention, managing emotions, developing and using conscience, using willpower).

Examples of functions housed in the thinking brain:

- Generates conscious, cognitive thought processes (although only about 5% of what goes on inside the brain may come to conscious awareness)

- Uses spoken, written, and gestured language, and engages in complex analysis

- Can process 125 bits of information and 40 bits of human speech per second

- Carries a sense of reflection and connection that can extend beyond the material world of bounded shapes into the abstract world

- Creates active mental picturing (versus passive mental picturing that is involved when watching TV, videos, and movies)

- Anticipates and plans for the future

- Contains an interest in and an impulse toward novelty

- Can fantasize , imagine, innovate, and cogitate about "what if"

- Stores information related to data important in society/culture (e.g., names, dates, numbers, labels) as well as data that contain emotional components

- Can evaluate, moderate, monitor, and redirect sensory reports

Minus another dog story, your **action brain** might feel like throwing this book across the room, while your **emotional brain** is ready to sob. But your **thinking brain**, fully engaged—although perhaps ready to explode—is saying, *Good stuff. Tell me more. This is helpful.*

Your thinking brain: Don't leave home without it. Phrased positively: Take your thinking brain *everywhere* with you—and use it by design.

Downshifting Phenomenon

When the going gets tough, a vehicle's automatic transmission shifts into a lower gear. You are driving up to Lake Tahoe and the road gets steep, it begins to rain, and traffic builds up. If it is working correctly, your vehicle will downshift to second or even first gear—as far as it needs to go in order to *get through.* If driving conditions are so severe that your vehicle can't make it in first gear, you'll likely stall.

 Now, picture the reverse situation. The road levels out, the rain stops, and traffic disperses. Your vehicle will now upshift to third gear. If it fails to upshift, your vehicle can be a hazard on the highway (e.g., traveling too slowly), require additional time and fuel to reach your destination, or the engine may fail and you will need to call a tow truck.

A similar situation can occur in the brain during situations of trauma, crisis, or fear. According to Dalip Singh, author of the book *Emotional Intelligence at Work*, stress and threat cause the brain to downshift, which reduces the opportunity for neuron growth and causes learning to be inhibited.

In other words, the brain focuses its attention and energy toward lower brain layers in an attempt to access responses and reactions that are perceived to be safer or that are believed to promote safety. The metaphor of "downshifting" applies very well to explain this process.

It's no surprise, therefore, that when a student becomes stressed-out in a classroom (say before a test or oral presentation), he/she may have trouble with cognitive activities. "I can't think!" (probably cannot) is often the response. Sometimes a behavioral response such as "fight-or-flight" seems an easy way out.

Reward and punishment-based systems—at school, home or the workplace—stifle creativity and increase confrontation. "Thinking" of positive ways to handle the stress is nearly impossible.

After all, how can people speed up a project or accelerate positive behavior when the brain has downshifted from all the stress? Simple answer: they can't.

Downshifting results in an automatic shift of attention and energy away from the thinking brain layer towards the lower brain layers (action and emotion), all outside of conscious awareness. Think of it as a fast slide down a flight of stairs. It can happen in a nanosecond.

The emotional brain (2nd layer or gear) responds to the signals of danger provided by both the action brain (1st layer or gear) and the thinking brain (3rd layer or gear). Signals of danger could even include evaluation, criticism, and anxieties created in one's own imagination.

When you are insecure, anxious, undecided, and tense, the focus of attention can become divided among the three brain layers. You may think one thing, feel another, and act from impulses that are completely different from either of the other two.

Triggers for Downshifting

Evaluate your own experience and identify the types of situations most likely to trigger downshifting in *your* brain. Here are some examples to get you started:

Situations of trauma or crisis - Any situation that involves trauma or crisis (e.g., physical injury, death of a family member or friend, natural disaster, severe illness, hospitalization,  family member or friend in a war zone, bankruptcy, being fired, or you name it). The brain will automatically search its reactions options to find one or more that it hopes will help you feel safer.

Negative experiences - A negative experience of any type (e.g., being fired, going through a divorce, thinking negative thoughts, a sense of being shamed in front of others, dysfunctional patterns of living, abuse, addictive behaviors) shifts energy and attention from third gear to first. In fact, a negative signal from any part of the brain creates a negative response throughout the emotional system, which is then reflected throughout the entire body and brain.

Any type of fear - All forms of fear shift your attention and energy from the cerebrum to the brain stem. In such instances you don't have full access to your higher intelligence and therefore react on a more primitive level. The fear can be real (e.g., actual danger) or imaginary (e.g., fear of not fitting in, fear of failure). The emotion of fear is essential to living safely, because it alerts you to situations that could pose a danger.

Unfortunately, people tend to harbor many fears that have nothing to do with actual danger. Rather, it involves imaginary fear that may have its basis in past experience, self-esteem issues, learned patterns of negative thinking, unhealed woundedness, lack of specific skills related to living successfully, and (sometimes) a failure to leave childhood defense mechanisms behind and grow up into a mature adult.

As Toni Morrison put it in *Jazz:*

*Seeded in childhood, watered every day since,
fear had sprouted through her veins all her life.*

Evaluate Fear

If you recognize fearful thoughts, ask yourself
some questions and then pay attention to your
responses. Here are some suggestions:

(1) What do I fear? Is the fear real and valid?

If the answer is "yes," ask yourself what is the
worst thing that could happen? What is the
probability that the worst thing will happen? Can
you do anything about it? If yes, take appropriate
action related to the actual danger.

If the answer is "no" or if the fear is imaginary,
change the way you think. Negative thinking is
unlikely to improve the odds and can contribute
to illness. Recall a happy memory, identify
something to appreciate, or for which you are
thankful.

(2) Collect jokes, cartoons, riddles, humorous
anecdotes, and short stories that make you laugh.
Save them in a *laugh scrapbook.* Keep the
scrapbook handy and refer to it whenever you
need a mood-elevator. Laughter can help you
displace fear. It can also raise your serotonin
levels along with dopamine and endorphins.

Consequences of Downshifting

So your brain downshifted from third-level cognitive thinking to first-level reaction response when the humungous dog leapt over the fence and charged your way. Your feet knew exactly what to do, and chances are you didn't even have time to feel afraid. Until later when all danger was past! But even a good thing, taken to the extreme, can lose some of its helpfulness.

Communication can be hindered if the sender, the receiver, or both are in a downshifted state. Such information is important for professionals, whose services are often sought by individuals in crisis!

When downshifting is activated unnecessarily or sustained for a prolonged period, learning and development can be impaired in children—and thinking, learning, and decision-making can become faulty in adults. What does that mean?

- You may fail to recall what you heard (e.g., maybe less than 15% of what you heard during a crisis)

- You may have difficulty with cognitive learning and recall, miss seeing interconnectedness (e.g., fail to put two and two together), and may even accelerate the process of aging

- You may relapse into old learned beliefs and patterns of behavior, regardless of available information, or experience a reduced ability to take environmental and internal cues into consideration

- You may develop phobias (e.g., specific stimuli trigger inappropriate or exaggerated responses)

- You may experience altered immune system function and/or brain chemistry

Jan's Story

Jan's church took the weekly service seriously: attractive sanctuary, excellence in the arts, solid biblical teaching. But one weekend, just before the sermon, a group came out to perform a *silly* drama that (in Jan's opinion) bordered on sacrilegious. Instead of just waiting out the performance, she allowed herself to become fearful of what some of the other attendees would think. She could hardly wait for the skit to end.

But even when it did, Jan could barely concentrate on the sermon. Afterwards someone in her family commented on the "wonderful message." She was sorry to have missed it! Her down-shifted brain simply failed to perform cognitive functions.

Chris's story

When Chris lost his job, he took up a long-abandoned habit: smoking. Of course his thinking brain knew that was the worst possible decision, considering he had paid good money to participate in a program to help him beat the addiction to nicotine.

But when depression set in after a couple of 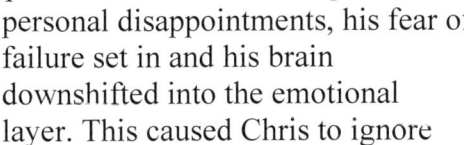 personal disappointments, his fear of failure set in and his brain downshifted into the emotional layer. This caused Chris to ignore his own common sense and he resumed a habit he thought he had conquered a decade before. (Where were his friends who promised to hold him accountable and help him through these tough times?) Hmmm.

Michelle's Story

"You look ten years younger," Greg told Michelle. No, she hadn't braved a face-lift or changed her make-up or gotten a new haircut. And Greg's eyesight was still 20/20.

 Instead, Michelle had been hired as a teacher after several years away from the classroom. Her other job had caused stress, fear, and worry up the proverbial ying-yang.

It had dishonored her brain's *bent*, putting her brain in extended-downshift mode. Teaching was her innate giftedness, and she was *so* glad to be back. No wonder she felt—and looked—younger. Who knew?

Strategies for Dealing with Personal Downshifting

Since brain downshifting is a natural brain phenomenon and kicks in automatically any time the brain perceives a lack of safety (e.g., trauma, crisis, fear) and will occur from time to time, how should a brain-smart person deal with it?

1 Know yourself and the symptoms you tend to exhibit when you are downshifted. For example, you may exhibit a tendency to:

- Become internally or externally defensive
- Overreact (big time)
- Isolate from others

Learning to recognize these symptoms quickly helps. You still can have access to the conscious third-layer thinking at some level even when your attention and energy is temporarily focused toward the lower brain layers.

Learn to talk to yourself: *Okay now, slow down. Take time to think. Maybe walking out (or screaming or being alone or punching him out) would not be my best option right now . . .*

Note: Experiencing feelings of sadness may be an appropriate response to a situation of loss and therefore may not necessarily indicate downshifting.

2 Define what you need in order to feel safe. The process of upshifting relates to the brain's perception of safety, which differs for different brains. Most people tend to feel some level of safety when they feel competent to handle basic developmental tasks in each area of life commensurate with their age, experience, and maturity level. What do you need most to feel safe? Here are some ideas to consider in six boundary areas:

- **Physical** – Freedom from physical violence and coercion by others, and a sense that you respect your own physical boundaries and those of others

- **Intellectual** – Freedom from having your mental boundaries being overrun by others, and a sense that you own and can exhibit your own abilities

- **Emotional** – Freedom from emotional harassment and abuse, and a sense that you are able to experience all your emotions while choosing the behaviors you will exhibit related to them

- **Social** – Freedom from being demeaned, shamed, or harassed in public or private situations, and a sense that you are safe with the other people involved

- **Sexual** – Freedom from coercion, harassment, or abuse, and a sense that you respect who you are innately as a member of your gender while according the same respect to others

- **Spiritual** – Freedom from ridicule or fear of punishment or shaming, a sense of awe or bliss, and a perception that you are able to live what has meaning for you (e.g., ethics, morals, humor, creativity, values, personal beliefs . . .)

3 Use pre-planned strategies to access high brain functions. Because your brain is so complex and capable, the good news is that you can think about and implement pre-planned strategies to help increase conscious awareness and high-level thinking whenever you identify that your brain is in a downshifted state.

Preplanned strategies can help you feel safer and thus enable you to access conscious awareness and higher-brain thinking instead of remaining in a reactive state. Following are some examples of preplanned strategies to help you jump-start this process (or to give you additional ideas if you already have given some thought to this).

Examples of such preplanned strategies

- Think of something humorous and laugh

- Engage in positive self-talk

- Walk around the block

- Exercise on a treadmill for a few minutes

- Mentally picture yourself in a safe, pleasant place

- Ask for help from a member of your support group

- Drink a glass of water

- Meditate or pray

- Sing or hum a tune

- Mentally imagine yourself exiting the first or second layer of the brain (wherever you perceive yourself to be at the moment), climbing up the outside of your brain until you reach the top (remember King Kong?), and then entering the third layer

- Make a mental contract to "deal with it later in the day"

How to Deal with Downshifting in Others

It should be patently obvious by now that to have a really cogent and cognitive conversation, both brains involved need to be upshifted—using the thinking-brain layer or third gear. When a communication situation is going poorly and you perceive "the light is on but nobody is home" (hopefully that doesn't describe your brain in that situation!), think downshifting.

While you can be a trigger for another brain to downshift, you cannot make another brain upshift.

Remember, downshifting is typically triggered when the brain doesn't feel "safe."

Therefore, if you sense that the brain of someone with whom you need to communicate is focused toward lower brain layers, do something to help that brain feel safer. This may result in it being able to upshift. Both brains really need to be upshifted if communication is going to be carried out at the conscious cognitive brain level.

 There are a number of strategies you can implement to help another brain *feel safer,* in the hope that this will make it easier for that brain to upshift if it chooses to do so. Here are four to consider.

193

1 Use short, simple, positive statements

Some believe that a portion of the emotional-brain layer (second gear) rarely matures beyond the emotional age of a 4 or 5 year-old child. Think about the ways in which you communicate with a child that age (e.g., typically short, simple instruction). For an adult with a brain in a downshifted state, that same style of communication works best.

The subconscious readily understands positives. Positive comments are a one-step process for the subconscious, which has more difficulty with negatives. When the subconscious layers try to process negatives (e.g., *Don't touch the stove!)*, the brain initially pictures touching the stove and tends to miss the word *don't.* It would be more effective to say, "Keep your hands away from the stove." Use positive, present tense words that all brain layers can perceive.

2 Use congruent communication to avoid sending mixed messages.

Studies have shown the way in which the message content is transmitted in a two-party communication:
- 7-10% through actual words
- 15-38% through voice tonality (e.g., sound, pitch, inflection, rate of speech)
- 55-75% through nonverbal communication

Therefore, in order for communication to be clear and effective and to avoid giving "mixed messages" your words, voice tonality, and nonverbals must be congruent—in harmony and coinciding with each other.

3 Avoid using the word *why.*

In the English language the word *why* can be perceived as stressful or threatening. It can trigger thoughts of *Oh-oh, I did it wrong* or *I'm afraid he/she will be mad at me because I did such and such or because I did not do such and such.* That can cause sufficient fear in the brain to trigger downshifting.

Try using different words to elicit the needed information—words that are less likely to trigger a sense of apprehension or fear.

Try these phrases instead:

- What did you want to happen?

- When you made this choice, what did you think might happen?

- Would a different choice have resulted in different outcomes?

- What could you do differently next time, or in the future?

4 Implement any or all of the following techniques:

- If the other individual is sitting down, sit down when conversing in order to be at his/her eye level

- Solicit the other person's input

- Communicate in a reflexive style (e.g., mirror the other person's words and communication style, whether Auditory, Visual, or Kinesthetic)

- Encourage the other person to participate in making decisions.

- Allow the other person to choose between two or more options

Note: With some thought you can usually provide an opportunity for the individual to exercise some control over at least part of the activity if not over the entire activity—the brain tends to feel safer when it can make a decision or when it perceives it has some control over something.

One More Caveat

Living a high-level wellness lifestyle can go a long way toward preventing periods of exhaustion. For every period of exhaustion, your brain will likely experience a corresponding period of depression.

While depression in and of itself may not be a trigger for downshifting, it can drain your energy and increase your risk of being challenged in areas that are difficult for you and are energy intensive.

Remember: downshifting is a natural and valuable brain phenomenon. But when used frequently and/or inappropriately it can have undesirable consequences. Used appropriately it can help you be "safer" in everyday living.

*Since your brain is your bottom line,
use it by design for success.*

In other words:

Honor the ***bent*** to avoid the ***dent.***

197

Point To Ponder

Everything can be taken from us but one thing—the last of the human freedoms—to choose one's attitude in any given circumstance.

—Viktor Frankl

Chapter Nine

STRESS: The Good, the Bad—and the *Good?*

The way I see it, I can choose to let stress control my life or allow life to control my stress.

Sandy Setterberg,
Flight attendant U.S. Airways

Y ou've heard of a *stress fracture* in a bone? A *stress test* to identify heart problems? How about a test in school that caused stress (as in *calculus exam* or *public speaking test*)?

Some type of stress exists at all levels of life because simply being alive requires the brain and body to continually adapt. Simply turning the pages of this book causes some stress because it requires parts of your body to adapt to change.

Yes, stress is part of living. In fact, the absence of stress is death! When your brain and body can no longer respond to demands for change, you are history. Until then, there is a great deal you can do in relation to the stressors in your life.

New Application

More than half a century ago, Dr. Hans Selye, of
Montreal's McGill University, attracted
worldwide attention when he borrowed the word
stress from the fields of physics and engineering
and applied it to human beings.

These days, the word *stress* is part of almost
everyone's vocabulary, especially as the global
village becomes more frenetic. Even though the
term is used freely, many people cannot clearly
explain what stress is, although they can often
describe the problems they believe stem from it.

Selye, often referred to as the *father of
stress management theory*, compared
reserves of energy to an inherited fortune socked
away in a bank account from which a person
could make withdrawals. When the account was
empty, the person was out of money.

There is some validity to that metaphor. The
good news is that today's researchers now
believe that a high-level-wellness lifestyle can
help you deposit energy back into your energy-
bank (so to speak), at least to some degree.

In other words, you can (to adapt Sandy's quote)
control your life and health—or your life can
control your health. Understanding that concept
and acting upon it can give you a freedom you
may never before have understood or utilized.

Stress Categories

In the 21st century, conversations often revolve around stress—its ups and its downs, its management strategies and their relative risk for success. Three categories of stress include *bents* and *dents:* Eustress, Misstress, and Distress.

 How you handle this trio in your everyday living can make all the difference in the world to your brain. (Maybe all the difference in the universe!)

Eustress – A beneficial *BENT*

The word *eustress* comes from the Greek root *eu,* meaning good. Think of eustress as stress that is desirable and healthy (and minus the negative feelings that so often seem to accompany distress and even mistress). Examples of may include marriage, childbirth, a promotion, vacation, continued education, even exercise. Many of these activities represent positive situations and accomplishments in one's life.

Eustress can trigger positive emotions and contribute to a sense of fulfillment. It can help you feel more mentally alert and focused, be more creative, and successfully master challenges. It can motivate you to discover new options for problem solving and to achieve your goals. It can bring joy.

Remember, however, that although you may consciously choose an activity or a course of action, to the degree that this requires your brain and body to adjust to a change, you will experience some stress—eustress.

Distress – A negative *DENT*

The word *distress* comes from the Latin root *dis,* meaning not desirable. Distress can be defined as unpleasant, negative, damaging stress—stimuli that, over time, can interfere with your ability to concentrate, focus, perform, and work at peak efficiency.

Distress is a relative concept. The perception of its impact can vary according to one's gender, cultural conditioning, sensory-system preference, extroversion/introversion ratio, and innate brain lead, to name just a few. After all, one person's pleasure may be another's poison, as the old saying goes.

Regardless, the bad news is that unmanaged, distress can kill—brain cells. In a state of distress, there is no true relaxation between one stressful episode and the next. The systems that stimulate the production of adrenalin, noradrenalin, and cortisone are stuck in the *on* position, so to speak, a scenario often linked with mental, emotional, and physical ailments.

Examples of undesirable stress are relatively easy to identify: bankruptcy, accidents, divorce (although sometimes this can result in eustress), miscarriage, burglary to your home or office, layoffs, fires, bereavement, recession, hurricanes, floods, and terrorism. You get the idea.

In general, think of *distress* as something you would definitely prefer to avoid!

Misstress – Beware this hidden *DENT*

The word *misstress* can be defined as hidden or unrecognized stress—stimuli and factors that most people tend to mislabel if they identify them at all. The prefix "*mis*" is an abbreviation of the Latin root *minus* meaning *less*.

Think of misstress as a whole host of little hassles often considered relatively minor or unimportant. But collectively . . .

On the surface, one might think that misstress is less harmful than distress. Not necessarily so. The greatest toll from stress may not come from the major traumatic changes or misfortunes in life that can be labeled rather obviously as distress. Rather, the greatest toll may result from misstress, those albeit minor annoyances that seem to happen rather frequently, such as:

- Getting stuck in traffic (not again) or long commutes to and from work

- Trying to lose those few extra pounds over and over again (big sigh here)

- Having a flat tire (is AAA paid up?)

- Misplacing the car keys (where *DID* I leave them this time?)

The unrecognized or hidden stress of *misstress* can take a huge toll. For example:

- Lack of sufficient amounts of sleep

- Failure to engage in regular physical exercise

- Negative mindset and/or negative self-talk styles

- Dehydration due to insufficient water intake

- Lack of nutritional food or poor eating habits. Remember that the word *stressed* is *desserts* spelled backwards. (More often than not, one leads to the other!)

- Technostress. That's a relatively new one! It refers to spending long periods of time sitting in front of a computer without taking regular breaks.

Stress-Brain Connection

Even if you're convinced that stress is the direct cause of your headache or shoulder tension, and you suspect it's connected to your indigestion and acne, you might question whether it affects your brain function. Read this carefully—then think again.

All stressors interact with the brain, the nucleus of your being. Messages move out from the brain through the endocrine system to the immune system and back to the brain.

Stress affects your brain!

As outlined in Hafen's book *Mind/Body Health*, the brain is usually the first body system to recognize a stressor. It reacts with split-second timing to instruct the rest of the body how to adjust. In fact, the brain can stimulate a "stress reaction" for as long as 72 hours after a traumatic incident.

Studies have shown that chronic stress can destroy brain cells. Who has an extra brain cell to lose? (Since basically you *are* your brain, it pays to hang onto all your brain cells for as long as you possibly can.)

When confronted with a stressor, human beings tend to initiate one of three basic reaction forms:

- Fight/Flight
- Tend/Befriend
- Conserve/Withdraw

Fight/Flight (F/F)

You have likely heard of the Fight/Flight reaction form. This basic *fight 'em or fall back* option is designed for rapid on/off action to help manage situations—when you think you can be successful or win!

The F/F reaction form (more likely to be activated by male brains) can be triggered by actual or potential threats, exertion, embarrassment, emotions such as fear/rage, and the person's own perception.

When F/F is triggered, hormones such as adrenalin flood the body within thirty seconds and the physiological effects are felt within about two minutes. In an emergency, that could be a life-saving *bent.*

However, F/F was never designed for chronic stress. Beware the potential *dents* from repeated triggering of F/F that can lead to high blood pressure, heart trouble, strokes, ulcers, and a host of other undesirable physical, emotional, mental, social, or spiritual side effects.

The body is able to return to homeostasis (e.g., rebalance itself from the hormonal effects of one episode of F/F) in approximately 18-24 hours. The good news here is that physical exercise can speed the rebalancing process.

Tend/Befriend (T/B)

You may not have heard of Tend/Befriend reaction form. Preliminary findings by UCLA researchers, including Dr. Shelley Taylor, suggest that females are more prone to activate T/B than F/F when stressors mount.

That is, females typically try to protect and nurture those who are important to them ("Tend") and turn to a social network of supportive females ("Befriend").

 The T/B response may have its basis in the secretion of oxytocin, a powerful hormone produced in the brain and distributed by the pituitary gland. Oxytocin is secreted at high levels in women during childbirth. It is also produced in both genders by stress and exerts a calming influence.

However, oxytocin appears to be enhanced by estrogen (higher levels in females) and diminished by androgens (higher levels in males).

Conserve/Withdraw (C/W)

The Conserve/Withdraw reaction form was designed to conserve energy and help you survive in situations where you perceive you cannot be successful or win.

The physiological changes are basically opposite from those generated during the Fight/Flight reaction form. Conserve/Withdraw represents a sort of "sit it out" approach. Metaphorically, some have described this process as one of hibernation. You just wait it out and hope things will improve, hope for the best.

Unfortunately, physical exercise is not believed to speed the rebalancing process after C/W is triggered.

C/W is stimulated by system overwhelm, unusual fear (real or imagined), a sense of hopelessness or helplessness, bereavement, and the spin you put on the event or situation.

Repeated triggering of C/W can lead to depression. Individuals who are depressed due to the repeated triggering of C/W tend to move through a predictable cycle of negative self-talk. The pattern is often referred to as Internal Stable Globalization or ISG for short.

Have you ever made a mistake and heard your brain running this cycle of self-talk?

For example, you do or say something you wish had not happened. ISG goes like this:

- **I**nternalize – you go *inside* mentally and say "I have done it wrong"

- **S**tabilize – you make this perception *stable* by saying, "I always do it wrong; I never do it right"

- **G**lobalize – you *apply* this perception generally by saying "I cannot do anything right"

As with many other patterns of behavior, the ISG cycle of negative self-talk is learned. Therefore, it can be *unlearned.* You can develop a positive mindset and an affirming communication style. It begins with you and your brain.

Break the Stress Cycle

Begin by identifying your own stress symptoms (e.g., nausea, insomnia, headaches, illnesses).

Then list your primary stressors (e.g., substances, emotions, processes, expectations, persons).

Finally, figure out your stress patterns (e.g., do you exhibit stress symptoms around specific stressors, at specific times of the day, in connection with specific holidays or days of the week, or when around specific individuals?)

Once you have this knowledge— and knowledge is power—choose to break free of the stress handcuffs. Use a combination of activities to interrupt and detonate the stress cycle. These can include exercise, meditation, massage, a change of activities, or even humor.

Following are three examples:

1. **Implement The QR** – Dr. Charles F. Stroebel, author of *QR, The Quieting Reflex,* designed this strategy to break the stress cycle. As soon as you recognize any tension, respond using the QR:

   - Smile to counter facial tension and alter the brain's neurochemistry

   - Tell your brain and body to be alert but calm and even amused

   - Breathe deeply and easily to increase the level of oxygen at the cellular level

   - Exhale and allow your body muscles to go limp as you feel warmth flowing through your body to your toes

   - Resume your normal activity

   Most people can smile, talk, and breathe. It doesn't get much easier than that!

2. **Live the 20:80 Rule** - It has been said that stressors generally interact with the brain in a predictable ratio sometimes referred to as another application of the 20:80 Rule.

The impetus for the 20:80 rule has been attributed to a man named Epictetus. This Greek Stoic Philosopher born c. 55 AD believed that it's not what happens to you, but how you react to it that matters.

In more modern times that philosophy has been turned into the 20:80 Rule. Briefly it states that:

- 20% of the negative effect to your brain and body is due to the stressor

- 80% of the adverse effect is due to what you think about the stressor and the credibility you give to it

Therefore, while you may be unable to control the 20%, you can have control over the 80% because you create the spin you put on the event.

Marli, a woman who applied the 20:80 Rule while traveling, recently shared her experience by e-mail.

Marli's Story

"I recently heard Dr. Taylor speak at an Elderhostel event, enjoyed her presentations very much, and learned a lot! On my journey back to Alaska I had my first opportunity to practice the 20:80 Rule.

"Arriving at the airport around 1:00 p.m. for a 2:30 p.m. flight, I discovered that my flight had been cancelled. My new reservations now indicated that I was to leave at 9:00 pm but (so sorry) connecting flights were unavailable. That clearly was not going to work for me. After some persistence and some additional searching, the reservation agent found a flight leaving from an airport located about a two-hour drive away. Fortunately, a shuttle was available.

"The shuttle van picked me up and I asked the driver if he could get me to the new airport in time for me to catch my flight. His response was, "I can try."

"So I thought of what I had learned at the seminar. Buckling on my seatbelt, I took a deep breath, got out my Sudoku puzzles and started to work on them.

"Looking at me through the rear-view mirror, the driver said, "You are so calm. Most of my passengers would be highly agitated if not yelling at this point in their travels!

"I shared information about the 20:80 Rule, outlined some of the stress management techniques I had learned, described how cortisol has a deleterious effect on one's brain and body, and thanked him for doing the best he could to get me to the church (oops, the airport) on time. I could not ask for more.

 "That triggered a very interesting conversation that lasted all the way to the airport. I learned a lot about business enterprises that were previously unknown to me. And I made my flight with time to spare. Vive la 20:80 Rule!"

Actually, Vive Marli's practical application of the 20:80 Rule!

3. **Develop a Positive Mindset** - A positive mindset involves giving yourself permission to succeed, regularly rehearsing positive behaviors, and creating specific action plans for stress management. Learn to speak to yourself in short, positive, present-tense phrases: *Way to go! Nice job! I'm doing it successfully. I thought I could! Watch this*!

   Many people sabotage themselves and contribute to their own problems because of the way they think. If you have an *enemy outpost* of negativity inside your mind, get rid of it.

This is stated so succinctly in the title of Peter McWilliam's book, *You Can't Afford the Luxury of a Single Negative Thought.* Stated in a positive style the title could be, *A Single Negative Thought Can Derail You!*

Does that mean you can choose never to have a negative thought again? Not likely. You can choose to recognize negative thoughts quickly, however, and change them immediately.

 According to Wikipedia, the philosophy espoused by the Greek Philosopher Epictetus influenced one of the Roman Emperors, Marcus Aurelius: "Aurelius quotes from Epictetus repeatedly in his own work, *Meditations*, written during his campaigns in central Europe." Marcus Aurelius said, *Your life is what your thoughts make of it.* That's shades of the 20:80 Rule.

Choose to cultivate a good sense of humor, and learn to laugh at yourself and at the vagaries of life. Studies have shown that very happy people laugh several hundred times a day. How many times a day do you laugh?

Practice mindful thanksgiving. Affirm what is positive in your life. As the old proverb states: *A grateful heart nourishes the bones.*

Jerry's Story

Jerry, a very successful business man, encouraged new recruits to think positively, saying, "Every time I become aware of a negative thought floating through my mind, I have learned to reach up metaphorically and turn the volume down." Jerry said that in his case, sometimes the "voice" was familiar (e.g., an aunt from childhood, a teacher from adolescence, an irritated parent), and oh the pleasure he felt to just turn it down and tune it out.

In addition, Jerry explained, "I immediately follow the negative thought with a positive one." For example, one day Jerry had tripped on the curb and the first words out of his mouth had been, "Yep, Buster. Mother was right. You are *so* clumsy!"

Jerry caught his self-talk immediately, laughed, and said aloud: "Well, Buster, thank heavens you stay on your feet most of the time. Your body managed to right itself quickly and save the knees in your new suit! Bravo!"

Interestingly enough, at the annual meeting Jerry reported his observations: new recruits who already had a positive mindset, or who put in the time and effort to develop one, tended consistently to be more successful in the long term than those who did not.

Fool-Hardy or Stress-Hardy?

Some people appear to be less affected by
stressful situations and seem more resilient in
adjusting to change. This quality has been
dubbed *stress-hardiness*. Several characteristics
have been identified in those who have been
judged to be stress-hardy. When you become one
of the so-called hardy people, you can cope quite
successfully with even high-stress situations
because you have modified your attitude and are
living *The Three Cs*. These are:

Control

You perceive you have a measure of power
over your life and are realistic in your
perception of what can be controlled. You
know you cannot control every detail in life,
but you know where you do have control and
are less likely to become ill under stress.

Challenge

You tend to perceive change as a challenge
rather than a threat and enjoy the challenge.
Change is inevitable. You are alert for
opportunities created by sudden changes.
When change is viewed as a threat, stress
levels rise. By viewing change as a
challenge, you may be able to minimize
some of the negative side-effects often
associated with stress.

Commitment

A strong sense of commitment allows you to see problems through—without being too disrupted or immobilized by stress. You reduce your risk of suffering from stress by doing what you really want to do at least some of the time. You make time to engage in activities that promote creativity and that reflect your own uniqueness.

Your Stories . . .

Life and living are all about *stories.* Many "happily-ever-after" stories are *yours*, just waiting to be lived and to be told. You have many personal stories—past, present, and future. Watch for them, recall them, discuss them, journal them, repeat them, and celebrate them.

The Bottom Line

Remember, if you are experiencing stress, you are alive. That can't be all bad, since the absence of stress is death. And learning how to identify and manage stressors effectively is all good. Aim to prevent or get rid of *distress* whenever possible. Take steps to reduce the amount of *misstress* in your life. And, above all, embrace and enjoy the *eustress*!

Point To Ponder

Every good mood you experience is your decision, and so is every bad mood. Everything you do in anger is your decision, and so is everything you do with love and compassion.

—Ralph Marston

Chapter Ten

The Powerful *Bents* and *Dents* of Emotional Intelligence (EQ)

I asked you what you were feeling, Harry.
"I'm really hungry for some chicken"
is not a feeling.

—Overheard at a July 4th picnic

Not long ago, just out of curiosity (and with this chapter in mind), we asked a friend about his educational history. The answer came swift and detailed. Then his spiritual history, where he was a bit more vague, but clearly had a timeline. Then his emotional history. At that question, there was simply a blank stare.

Maybe the man *has* no emotions, you say? No, he's been seen to cry at a missed Vikings field-goal attempt.

Perhaps more than anything else in this book so far is the importance of recognizing your emotional bent. There is one, you know.

Your brain is *one of a kind*. Not only do you begin life with a unique brain, every thought you think and every behavior you exhibits alters brain structure. Since no one else thinks your identical thoughts or exhibits your identical behavior, your brain can actually become even more different as you age.

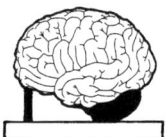 Because of this, no two brains are believed to be identical in structure, function, or perception, not even the brain of identical twins. This means that you can choose to avoid becoming defensive about the comments or opinions offered by another person—they only reflect that brain's perspective!

It also means that you can choose to avoid foolish argument and meaningless controversy. When people argue, especially when they become emotionally invested in the outcome and the intensity of the conversation escalates, you can be relatively sure that at least one of the brains "thinks it really knows." And if it just talks louder and longer and maybe throws in some coercion and a few pejoratives, that other "so-and-so brain" will finally get it. Not so.

As the old proverb goes:

> *A brain convinced against its will is*
> *of the same opinion still . . .*

Emotional Quotient (EQ)

Learning to effectively manage your emotions and feelings can pay exponential dividends. It is critical to success in business, to your state of health and wellness, to say nothing of your personal life and relationships.

Many people try to manage their emotions using strategies based on attitudes and beliefs typically absorbed prior to the age of five. While these strategies might have worked in childhood, they may work less well in adulthood and, in some cases, can be an actual hindrance.

Institutions (and prisons!) are filled with people who could not handle their emotions effectively and appropriately, whereas those who possess a high level of emotional intelligence are generally healthier, less depressed, more productive, and have more functional and rewarding relationships.

Emotional Intelligence is tied in closely with your brain's *bent*. In fact, EQ is the capacity to use your emotions effectively—to bring intelligence to them, if you will. It involves the ability to identify, learn from, remember, utilize, communicate, and understand emotions in an appropriate manner.

Never Too Late for EQ

According to authors Cooper and Sawaf (1998) in their book *Executive EQ – Emotional Intelligence in Leadership and Organizations,* EQ is a learned intelligence. It involves a set of acquired skills and measurable competencies that can be developed and improved at any age.

Key EQ skills include:

- Curiosity
- Logic
- Creativity
- Leadership
- Cooperation and Collaboration
- Organizational Awareness
- Customer Service Orientation
- Organizational Skills
- Communication Skills

EQ Caveats

You are in a much better position to make conscious choices about how you want to manage your emotions and feelings, your actions, and your behaviors when you:

- Are able to differentiate between your emotions and feelings, label each accurately, and recognize what your emotions are trying to tell you

- Have identified your emotional history, including the emotional atmosphere(s) you experienced during childhood and adolescence, and some of the factors that have contributed to your present emotional tone

- Know that while you may not be able to control the surfacing of every emotion, you can control the feelings you maintain related to the emotion, the actions you select, and the behaviors you choose to exhibit

- Internalize that if you want to change the way you feel, you need to change the way you think (because feelings follow thoughts)

Understanding something about emotions in general (and the ways in which you tend to deal with them) offers you the opportunity to consciously select appropriate and efficacious behaviors for a given situation. As with everything else in life, honing these skills requires time, energy, commitment, and practice. There's no time like the present to begin.

Daniel Goleman, author of the book *Working with Emotional Intelligence,* said:

We are being judged by a new yardstick: not just how smart we are, or by our training and expertise, but also by how well we handle ourselves and each other.

Collaboration: Group EQ

People regularly need to collaborate with others. As such you have a group IQ—the sum total of talents and skills of all those involved.

How well the group accomplishes their task, however, will be largely determined by the level of group EQ—working effectively to achieve social harmony and meaningful collaboration.

Are you seeing how the *bent* and *dent* metaphors could play in here? Author Daniel Goldman has also stated:

The single most important element in group intelligence, is not the average IQ in the academic sense, but rather in terms of emotional intelligence.

 Take two groups, one that has high EQ and the other with low EQ. All things being equal, the group that has the ability to harmonize and collaborate will tend to be more successful. They will out-produce the other group every time.

What is the difference? While a group may be no *smarter* than the sum total of all their strengths, the group can be much *dumber* by failing to recognize, affirm, and encourage members to share their brain-giftedness.

Perceiving Emotions

 Human beings vary tremendously in their ability to perceive their own emotions and those of others. They also vary in their ability to identify, articulate, and manage emotions. They also differ in their interest and commitment related to raising their level of EQ.

Juliette's story

Due to circumstances beyond their control, Juliette's parents found themselves out of a job, out of a home, and out of money. Not knowing what else to do, they placed Juliette in an orphanage on her fifth birthday, promising they would return for her when they had saved enough money to put the family together again.

It was more than 18 months before they returned to claim little Juliette. The experience left her brain quite traumatized. Indeed she seemed to stop growing emotionally although she continued to grow physically into a beautiful young woman.

For the remainder of her life, whenever a stressful situation occurred, Juliette responded very childishly. The level of her emotional intelligence never approached that of either her IQ level or her chronological age.

High EQ Matters

In his book *Emotional Intelligence,* Author Dr. Daniel Goleman estimates that IQ, at best, probably contributes about 20% to the factors that help determine a person's life success.

EQ, on the other hand, can be much more powerful and likely contributes 80% or more to one's success in life.

This can help to explain the reason that some individuals with reportedly very high IQs realize very little overall success in life—their EQ is not nearly as high as their IQ.

Take a moment to think of someone you know or have known who appears to exercise little if any control over his or her emotions or resulting behaviors. Does his or her EQ level match their chronological age? How does that affect relationships? Self-esteem? Success?

Emotional intelligence, managing emotions optimally, is a learned skill. Typically it is absorbed by observing caregivers and role models. Unfortunately, not everyone learned that skill growing up. If your caregivers and role models possessed high levels of EQ you likely got a jump-start on the process.

If that were not the case, you may have grown up without developing the tools necessary to manage emotions appropriately and effectively. In such a case, you will have to work harder to do so in adulthood. This includes identifying triggers that can tie you in knots emotionally and negatively impact your business and work situations as well as your personal life.

And it means learning effective strategies for identifying and managing emotions.

Gender Differences

The joke that "males never remember marital spats and females never forget . . ." is now backed up by research. Studies show that women tend to recall emotional events better than men.

According to Turhan Carili, assistant professor of psychology at State University of New York Stony Brook, "The wiring of emotional experience and the coding of that experience into memory is much more tightly integrated in women than in men." This study may also shed light on reasons that clinical depression is more common in women.

Females are usually more comfortable expressing emotions and feelings in words. Due to their more generalized thought-processing style, females tend to have less difficulty combining thinking and feeling states.

Females have often been socialized to be more comfortable expressing emotions through tears, causing them to appear more sensitive. Their challenge is to avoid perpetually indulging negative feelings and brooding endlessly over hurtful incidents. They may need to be encouraged to take action. Almost any action can help, such as physical exercise.

As a group, males are generally reluctant to verbalize emotions and feelings, and are more likely to express them through actions rather than words. They may have more difficulty shifting from thinking to feeling states as their brain function is more lateralized (e.g., hemispheres can act more independently).

Preliminary research has shown that the amygdalae (structures in the second brain layer that have to do with emotions and memory) grow more quickly in boys than in girls. This means that males do experience deep emotion, especially those who have a right-brained preference. Many males have the potential for being equally or more sensitive as compared to females, but males haven't always learned to be in touch with their emotions or how to articulate them appropriately.

Because of societal expectations that males should remain in control of their emotions (essentially be silent), males may fail to articulate their feelings. They are more likely to act-out their emotions and feelings (e.g., crash the car, get drunk, kick the cat, and engage in high-risk or violent behaviors). They need to learn to communicate verbally, articulate emotions and feelings, and act in a safe and appropriate manner.

Both males and females need to learn to identify emotions and feelings accurately. If they can't tell the difference between being angry or hungry, they may eat whenever they are upset— and then they could have more to be upset about.

Get a Grip on Your Emotions

EQ has as much to do with knowing when and how to express emotions appropriately as it does with managing your behaviors around those emotions.

Sigdal Barsade performed an experiment at Yale University. He recruited a group of volunteers to play the role of business managers who had come together in groups to allocate bonuses to their subordinates.

A trained actor was planted among the groups. The actor always spoke first. In some groups the actor projected cheerful enthusiasm, in others relaxed warmth, in others depressed sluggishness, and in still others hostile irritability.

The results indicated that the actor was able to infect the group with his emotions. Positive emotions led to improved cooperation, fairness, and overall group performance. In fact, objective measures indicated that the cheerful groups were better able to distribute the money fairly and in a way that significantly helped the organization.

Similar findings have been reported from the field. Bachman found that the most effective leaders in the US Navy were warmer, more outgoing, emotionally expressive, dramatic, and sociable. Would you even expect to find such leaders in the military?

Powerful Signals

Emotions are powerful and are the link to bring subconscious information to conscious awareness. They can over-ride conscious thought in a nanosecond unless you are emotionally mature, and even then it can be a challenge. The stimulus that triggers an emotion may be something in the external environment or in one's own internal environment.

Emotions are physiological changes that occur in response to a stimulus or trigger. They are triggered by what Dr. Candace Pert refers to as molecules of emotions—neuropeptides and receptor molecules—that serve both to link and to unify the brain and body, connecting the subconscious with the conscious.

Emotions are gifts of information. They arise simultaneously in every cell in your brain and body. These cellular signals (flags) are designed to get your attention, provide vital information, and generate energy so you can take appropriate action. They also add safety, color, and enjoyment to life and can be experienced without being acted upon.

Can you even imagine having no emotions?

Just in case you're wondering if there is a dedicated center for emotions in the brain, the answer is probably not. Different regions make differing contributions. Examples follow:

- Emotional impulses are believed to arise in the second brain layer, in the portion of the brain that houses the hippocampus (responsible for recording and recalling—much as an Internet search engine—your autobiographical memories such as what you ate for dinner yesterday or your first day on the new job)

- The third brain layer is thought to be responsible for managing and expressing emotion including functions of identification, interpretation, cognitive thought processing, decision-making, and the creating of feelings

- The frontal left lobe appears to be activated when joy is experienced (and perhaps at some level for anger, fear, and sadness)

- The right frontal lobe appears to be activated when the protective emotions are experienced: anger, fear, and sadness

- The left hemisphere controls fine motor movements that are not as key in initiating the fight/flight response to stressors

- The right hemisphere controls the larger motor functions of the arms and legs that are needed to initiate and take action related to the fight/flight response

- The right posterior lobes appear to perceive emotions (in the self and in others) and tend to be the most empathetic

According to Dr. Pert, molecules of emotion create altered states of consciousness, each of which comes with different behavioral patterns, memories, postures, facial expressions, and levels of information substances.

Pert has postulated that there may even be specific neuropeptide(s), brain chemicals that impact mood, associated with each core emotion.

Emotional Expression—To Do or Not to Do . . .

 There has been a great deal of hype about the way in which emotions *should* be expressed. The pendulum has often swung wildly from repressing all emotion to emoting everything. Neither, in fact, is desirable; the preferred position is somewhere in between the two extremes.

- **Bottle 'em up** - This represents an undesirable response or choice. Repressed or suppressed emotions tend to build up pressure and can erupt at some future time

- **Let 'em all hang out** - This also represents an undesirable response or choice, even if it is opposite from the *Bottle 'em up* position. One hundred and eighty degrees from dysfunctional is still dysfunctional. Catharsis, so-called, can escalate emotional intensity, lead to addictive behaviors, and have a negative outcome overall

- **Management and moderation** - This is the preferred position. Consciously identify and experience all emotion—and take appropriate action. This can run the gamut from silence or calm verbalization to taking physical action

Understanding how you tend to approach emotions and feelings gives you an opportunity to hone your management skills and to exhibit behaviors in a given situation that serve best.

Emotional Overreactions

Past unresolved loss can increase the intensity of your reaction to present episodes of loss. An overreaction may occur due to an accumulated slush fund of unresolved emotional pain.

When you react out of proportion, especially when the situation involves cross-gender communication, your overreaction often relates to the past.

Typically in situations of overreaction, something about the current situation reminds your brain of a past event (e.g., unhealed woundedness, unresolved grief event, abuse, shame, an event you hated, chronic anger about a situation or person) and brings the force of that pent-up emotion to bear on the present.

Understanding or figuring out reasons for an overreaction can be a gift if it serves as a clue to encourage you to become your own Sherlock Holmes and engage in some family-of-origin work. This can help you to avoid *shooting the messenger*.

It is important to refrain from blaming another person whose actions may simply have served as a trigger (so to speak) for your own memory processes.

Emotions and Feelings—Not Necessarily the Same

The development of EQ is enhanced when you understand the difference between emotions and feelings and make a commitment to manage both appropriately. Just that in and of itself will likely place you in a small, elite group of individuals on this planet—and put you light years ahead of most!

In the English language the words *emotions* and *feelings* frequently are used interchangeably, as synonyms for each other, the same adjectives often applied to each.

This is unfortunate because in terms of brain-function information, emotions and feelings are not synonymous. These words represent different concepts and differing states in the brain and body.

According to Dr. Zach Lynch in his article "Emotions in Art and the Brain" (published in *The Lancet* 2004), emotions and feelings are mediated by distinct neuronal systems in the brain.

Emotions are Inborn

 Although beliefs differ regarding the number of core emotions, clear scientific evidence exists that facial expressions registering specific core emotions are inborn and present during gestation. These include (at minimum) the emotions of joy, anger, fear, and sadness.

Core emotions are designed to help you become aware of specific sensory stimuli and to manage specific situations in life, thus they are all *positive*, although feelings and behaviors related to emotions are often mismanaged, or handled in a manner that results in a negative outcome.

Each emotion produces a specific state of consciousness complete with typical facial expressions, physiological markers, gestures, and actions. When in the grip of a strong emotion, you are essentially in a biochemically-altered state, if you will.

Core *Emotions*

No one knows how many emotions actually exist. Certainly there are dozens of names that could be applied to the same emotion. There are some core emotions, however, that are generally agreed upon.

Following is a list of core emotions along with their purposes and examples of undesirable outcomes that can result from mismanagement.

Euphoria (awe, elation, bliss)

Euphoria is a signal that something highly rewarding or pleasurable is happening. It provides energy to experience special moments that can add spice and excitement to your life.

Unmanaged, euphoria can prompt you to search for activities that provide a continual high, through direct or indirect self-medication that alters your neurochemistry (e.g., addictive behaviors).

Joy (happiness, delight, enthusiasm, felicity, general contentment, gladness)

Joy is a signal that all is going well in your life. It is a natural state of anti-depression hardwired into the brain. It provides energy to live life in all its fullness—balanced, contented, and productive.

The brain-body was designed to spend the majority of time at a position of joy. It was never designed to live in a state of euphoria anymore than in a state of anger, fear, or sadness.

In fact, joy is the only emotion that has no negative consequences when maintained over time.

Pseudo joy or false joy can lead to obsessions and compulsions, addictive behaviors, a sense of unreality, frustration, and depression.

Anger (rage, fury, indignation, bitterness, wrath, ire, hostility)

Anger is a signal that your boundaries have been breeched (e.g., physical, mental, emotional, sexual, spiritual). It provides energy to create and implement bona fide boundaries.

Without anger you may lack the motivation to take corrective action or you may begin to tolerate the intolerable.

Unmanaged, anger can lead to bitterness, illness, injury, and death. It may be one of the most misunderstood and misused emotions.

As Aristotle put it: "Anyone can become angry; that is easy. But to be angry with the right person, to the right degree, at the right time, for the right purpose, and in the right way, this is not easy."

Fear (fright, alarm, panic, terror, apprehension, dread)

 Fear is a signal of danger. It provides energy to take appropriate protective action. Without fear you may be unable to protect yourself adequately.

Unmanaged, fear can kill your ideas, undermine confidence, and escalate into phobias and/or immobilization.

Sadness (unhappiness, grief, somberness, regret, depression, downcast spirit)

Sadness is a signal that you have experienced a loss. It provides energy to grieve losses and recover. Without sadness you may be unable to grieve successfully.

Unmanaged, sadness can lead suppression of to immune function, depression, and/or immobility (even apathy). Chronic sadness or depression has been associated with a reduction in specific brain chemicals such as serotonin.

Feelings - *Wo-woo-wooo . . . Feelings*

Feelings represent a horse of a different color. As mentioned earlier, the word *feelings* is often (unfortunately) used as a synonym for emotions. But feelings actually represent a separate concept, although one that is closely connected with emotion.

Feelings are subjective interpretations that emerge from your cognitive processing of an emotion-eliciting state. This means that although you may not trigger your own emotions (although it is possible to do so by the thoughts you think), you do create the feelings you hang onto.

 Based on your preferences, learned habits, background, experiences, education, habits, perceptions, beliefs, and thought patterns (to name just a few), your brain tries to make sense of the physiological changes that resulted from the emotion that surfaced.

As Wayne Dyer puts it,

> *You can't have a feeling without first having a thought."*

Feelings follow thoughts. As such, to change the way you feel, change the way you think.

Emotions Staircase Model

The emotions staircase is a model that portrays core emotions as a series of steps. You can take a slide down to the bottom step in a nanosecond, depending what is going on around you and your response to it. Learning to climb back up to joy is often more of a conscious choice. With practice, you may be able to do this in a matter of minutes.

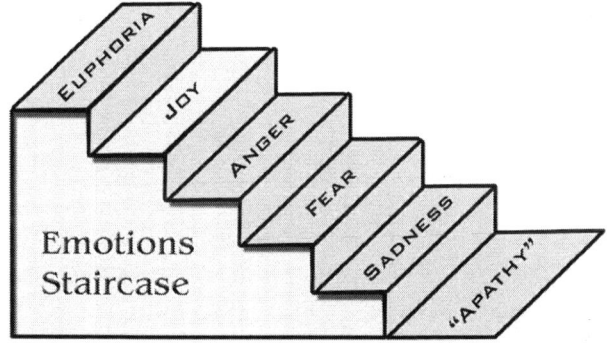

Beginning at the bottom, the first step represents sadness. The next step up represents fear, then anger, then joy, and at the very top is euphoria.

Apathy is portrayed at the very bottom of the Emotions Staircase. Apathy is probably not an emotion, but rather a position of emotional overwhelm and immobility, often due to a lack of understanding or skill level related to managing emotions and feelings.

Your Hypothetical Picnic Climb

How could this work for you? Let's say you were at the July 4th picnic engaging in conversation over traditional yummy food. Someone made a comment that represented a view very different from your own. Between bites you stated your opinion. Almost instantly, one of the other picnickers made a rather rude and judgmental comment. In a flash you took a slide down the emotions staircase. How do you know that? You recognize a desire to overreact and give that person a big piece of your mind.

So what do you do? First, you can avoid meaningless controversy and foolish argument. Realize that each brain only has its own opinion and let it go at that. Second, you can hold a conversation with yourself and talk yourself back up the stairs. Following is an example:

Walking up the Emotions Staircase

Ask: Where am I on the Emotions Staircase?

Answer: At sadness, because _____ said my opinion was ridiculous and that I was "just too stupid." I know I am as smart as most other people and that my brain just has a different opinion from _____.

Ask: How long do I want to stay at sadness?

Answer: I'm done. I'll step up to fear. I'm afraid someone else will say something hurtful to me like this again. However, I know that it is only their brain's opinion and I will choose if I want to believe their opinion or make it mine.

Ask: How long do I want to stay at fear?

Answer: No need to stay any longer. I'll move up to anger. I'm angry that someone would be so unkind in their comments. However, I know I can't control their comments, only my response to them. (Where is that 20:80 Rule?)

Ask: How long do I want to stay at anger?

Answer: Nada. Zip. Hey, I'm at joy! The lesson I've learned is that sticks and stones may break my bones but words will not hurt me long-term—unless I choose to allow that to happen.

Fortunately the staircase has no gates. You can continue to climb back up every time you take a slide down . . . because you're on a journey that's *only just begun.* With increased awareness of your own emotions and with more effective strategies for managing them, you can spend much more time at the "bent" of joy.

In fact, as you gain skill in this area, you may find yourself moving down to anger, fear, or sadness only when appropriate—and rather quickly walking back up to joy.

Point to Ponder

*To thine own self be true, and it must follow as
the night follows the day, thou
canst not then be false to anyone.*

—William Shakespeare

Chapter Eleven

Your Path—Finding the *Bent* in the Road

*If you begin to understand what you are
without trying to change it, then what you are
undergoes a transformation.*

—J. Krishnamurti

Anne's Story

Anne's eyes fluttered open and focused
uncertainly on her surroundings. Where was she?
The sight and sounds of the hospital room
gradually oriented her. *I'm so exhausted,* Anne
thought to herself. *I don't have the energy to face
this.*

Pneumonia. Again. How had she
gotten into this predicament?

Adaption.

The word popped into Anne's mind. It had
started a very long time ago, her pattern of
adapting. *Maybe even from birth*, she thought.

Trying desperately, even fervently, to juggle and satisfy the myriad expectations of family, school, church, friends, society, and work—and do it all perfectly . . .

And in the process Anne had pretty much ignored her own needs and self-care. No surprise, this is what it had gotten her. Another illness. Another hospitalization.

For the past decade Anne had managed a large county department. Her duties included writing grants, arguing budget allocations, and overseeing dozens of programs, scores of employees, and millions of dollars.

To all outward appearances Anne was very successful, but it had come at a very high price and she actually enjoyed very little of it. She had tried her best to conform to the strong work ethic that had been passed down to her from previous generations. An ethic that said: be a nice girl, be a good girl, don't be proud, follow the rules, work hard, worship faithfully, meditate/pray regularly, always value others before yourself, and everything will "come up roses" in the end.

But they had been wrong—oh so wrong.

Instead of roses, life was flat-out exhausting. Anne usually arrived home to collapse in bed for a few hours of fitful sleep. Then she'd crawl out from under the covers to do it all over again.

Periodically she would crash (no surprise). Often those crashes were accompanied by illness. Her annually-repeated bouts with pneumonia were one example. Sometimes her illnesses were accompanied by hospitalizations.

"If I live through this," Anne said aloud to no one in particular, "I'm going to learn everything I can about my brain and get serious about crafting a life that works for it."

Fast-forward twenty years. Anne survived and continues on the personal journey that began when her life nearly ended. She stopped adapting excessively, gradually quit trying to fit into everyone else's model and expectations for her life, and sought the path she should have been on in the first place—her own path. The results?

- Improved health and more energy

- Seemingly effortless productivity in some arenas

- More selective but very rewarding relationships

- Sheer *joy*

When others around her ask, "What's your secret?" her immediate response is, "Know who you are and live it. It's the only way to fly." And fly she does.

A Quick Review of *Bents* and *Dents*

This entire book has stressed the need to know yourself, to understand the advantages that have been built into your brain. Potentially you can be happier, healthier, and more successful by living out your brain's innate giftedness on a daily basis.

Going back to this book's beginning, **Chapters Two and Three** identified that your brain has a bent—a natural preference or advantage that impacts the way you process information. Understanding your own brain bent and matching the majority of your activities to what your brain does easily, can positively change your life. It can add life to your years and maybe years to your life.

While the concept is simple, it's not always easy to live out your innate giftedness against the backdrop of myriad expectations—from self, family, school, career, church, and society. But it's worth the work.

Chapter Four examined some important brain differences between the genders, although as members of the same species, human beings are really more alike than they are different. Being true to your own gender—yet understanding the other—is key for collaboration, improved mental health, and peaceful social coexistence.

Chapter Five reviewed extroversion, ambiversion, and introversion, noting that your brain is wired from birth for its innate position on the EAI Continuum. This position reflects the relative amounts of stimulation your brain craves or can handle before seeking relief.

Chapter Six introduced the sensory systems. Most brains have a unique sensory package that amounts to yet another personal preference. Unimpaired, your brain can process visual, auditory, and kinesthetic data, and does that much of the time. However, one type of stimuli likely registers in your brain more quickly and intensely. This preference impacts not only the way you learn, but also all your relationships.

Chapter Seven addressed adaption and provided examples of desirable versus undesirable adaption. Temporary adaption is useful and desirable and gives you options for short-term use. But for your mental and physical well-being, prolonged adaption is not your best option. Again, the concept is simple, but the ongoing application of the information on a daily basis can be a challenge.

Chapter Eight dealt with the *dent* that can come from your brain's response to trauma, crisis, or any type of fear—downshifting. This important chapter helps you understand a natural brain phenomenon. It can be oh so helpful when used appropriately and harmful when used inappropriately. It also provided tips for improving communication with others whose brains are in a downshifted state.

Chapter Nine dealt with stress, good and bad and hidden. You live in stress on this planet and it is critical to learn how to identify it, handle it, and even use it to your advantage.

Chapter Ten emphasized the importance of Emotional Intelligence and recognized that humans have emotional bents and dents. Understanding your emotional history could help you make a real breakthrough in healthy emotional living in the present.

And now, here in **Chapter Eleven**, you are ready to tie all the information together and ask yourself the all-important question: "Am I living authentically?"

Rephrased, this simply asks:

Do you know your brain's preferences, and have you matched at least 51% of your life's activities with your brain's innate energy advantage?

Many individuals have not achieved a desirable match between their innate preferences and their life activities—career endeavors, relationship roles, and recreational choices.

Is this a new problem? Evidently not. Over the centuries writers have spoken to the need of being true to one's self. The famous line from *Hamlet* is just one example, and more profound than Shakespeare probably realized. In our fast-paced and often frantic world, these words may even be truer or more applicable today.

Perhaps the most important factor in living a successful life by design is learning as much as possible about how your brain functions. After all, it is your identity! You cannot do without it, and it can never be replaced. No "stolen identity" when it comes to your brain—your greatest resource.

Gerald's Story

Gerald, a CEO for a large multi-state corporation, often challenged his department directors to view their jobs in a new way. He wanted them each to realize that every job has enjoyable parts and also dissatisfying parts. "It's like cooking," he would explain. "Occasionally you have to stop and do the dishes. Cooking is fun. Dishwashing isn't."

As you learn to live authentically, remember Gerald's metaphor and do more cooking—less dishwashing.

Reality Check

There is hope! If you identify your brain's innate preferences in four key areas (refer to the *"Who Am I?" Pyramid* Model on page three) and put into practice what you learn, the practical application of this knowledge can result in a more efficient use of your vital energy.

You may need to face uncomfortable realities. Are you in a career that doesn't even come close to matching your innate giftedness? If so, should you just up and quit?

Perhaps your sensory preference isn't being honored in your most significant relationship. Should you just walk away?

Maybe you are not being appreciated for your position on the gender continuum, or perhaps you are being shamed, if not punished, for your position on the EAI Continuum. Should you medicate your frustration and depression with alcohol, prescriptions, or some addictive behavior?

For each of the above options, read this carefully: No. Of course not. It would be a terrible mistake to quit, walk away, or self-medicate your frustration and depression with alcohol, prescriptions, or some addictive behavior. It would be beneficial to review each carefully and craft a long-term solution. Why?

Because this issue of mismatches is real, it is to be hoped that you'll take the time to identify mismatches in your life—and then create a plan for resolving them.

Quick Fix Opportunities

You may want to review the following strategies to help you plan a course of action. Think of them as temporary fixes to implement, tips that can assist you to get on with living a quality life as soon as possible.

First, begin to include activities in your life that honor your innate preferences. Or, if you've already started that, increase the number and frequency of those activities.

For example, if your job as an auditor doesn't match your innate preferences in the right frontal lobe and consequently is draining your energy, develop hobbies or extracurricular activities that do match. Pursue them after work, on weekends, in your discretionary moments. Revel in them.

Pay attention to how your brain and body feel as you engage in each activity, and move toward repeating those that help you feel your best. The options are endless. Here are just a few:

- Read adventures, travel, or personal-growth books; travel or watch travelogues

- Join a local community board and get involved with change

- Write poetry or short stories; join a creative writing club

- Travel—to places you've only dreamed about

- Sign up for a watercolor class

- Attend jazz concerts; if you play the sax, join a jazz band

- Create opportunities for spontaneity

If you are an elementary teacher but feel your giftedness relates more to systems orchestrated by the left posterior lobes, consider these options:

- Develop family or school traditions and act on them

- Play on a team that has rules and follows them; read stories about team sports

- Develop routines that you can follow

- Solve crossword puzzles

- Volunteer in a library

- Get season tickets to a sporting event

- Learn to knit or crochet

- Plan and take a packaged cruise

If you are a psychiatrist or counselor and find that eight-to-ten hours of one-to-one interaction is draining and that your brain bent is more aligned with left frontal-lobe functions, try one or more of these:

- Set specific financial goals and make decisions about investments

- Join a chess club, or some type of thinking competition

- Get involved with two-team sports, such as tennis or racquetball; try one-person activities like golf or jogging

- Try a home-improvement project

- Campaign for your favorite candidate during elections (if your brain leans toward extroversion)

- Chair a community board

- Read books about great leaders

- Study to increase the size of your vocabulary and join a debate club

If you are a department manager and discover that you are really more comfortable with activities that utilize functions from the right posterior lobes, try these on for size:

- Take a mini-vacation with your family and pets, or visit close friends, go on a picnic, or potluck in the back yard

- Get involved in a local drama group or join the community choir

- Join a community choir or orchestra

- Find friends or associates to exercise with on a regular basis

- Join a social club

- Read nonfiction nature books, biographies, or romances

- Learn how to speak a foreign language

- Hang out with a chef, interior decorator, or chaplain

Managing Stimulation

If your environment is too stimulating, take steps to carve out a niche for yourself where you can more effectively manage the amount of stimulation. Perhaps that is a room of your own or a private space somewhere in your home.

 If your environment isn't providing you with enough stimulation, up the ante. Use an iPod. Take breaks to exercise, connect with others, or catch up on the news. Be creative. Make new friends who share your brain bent, and develop hobbies that match what your brain does energy-efficiently. Do what you can—until it is financially responsible to make a career or lifestyle change.

That day could come sooner than you think—or perhaps never. But at least you are more brain-smart now and can make healthy adjustments.

Remember that a 100% match isn't the goal, and likely wouldn't be doable anyway. A majority match is both.

Janeen's Story

At one point during her teenage years, Janeen was grounded by her parents. (You know the drill.) It seemed like forever (even though the time period was brief) and "dreadfully unfair."

To give her something to do, her English-teacher father suggested she memorize Edgar Guest's poem entitled "Myself." Much to his surprise (the father's, not Guest's) she did.

The first stanza began:

> *I have to live with myself, and so*
> *I want to be fit for myself to know.*
> *I want to be able, as days go by,*
> *Always to look myself straight in the eye;*
> *I don't want to stand in the setting sun,*
> *And hate myself for things I've done.*

Of course, at the time, Janeen thought that last phrase ("things I've done") meant every teenager's favorite sins.

257

 Years went by and Janeen thought of the poem infrequently. One day, however, some of the words popped into her mind. And, as an ongoing student of emerging brain research, she began to perceive the poem in an entirely new light. She realized that it could speak to living authentically.

The words "I want to be fit for myself to know" could mean being who she was meant to be—innately. That's just plain honest.

Wanting to always "look myself straight in the eye" could mean honoring her brain's own unique giftedness. That's respect.

Not wanting to end life by hating one's self "for things I've done" now meant to Janeen that, in her twilight years, she wanted to avoid thinking or saying things such as:

- "I grew up wanting to be a teacher, but I never got the chance . . ."

- "I always wanted to dance, but now I think it's too late . . ."

- "I wish I would have entertained more, but my house was never in order . . ."

- "I would have loved to start my own business, but I didn't think I was smart enough . . ."

- "I spend years as a (you can fill in the blank _____) just because that's what I was told to do, but I never, ever enjoyed doing it . . ."

You get the idea.

When you come to the end of your time on this planet, it may not be the things you *did* that could cause you the most regret as much as the things you *didn't* do—the education or information you ignored, the choices you failed to make, the opportunities you were too fearful to seize, the travel you never took, the healthy risks you refused to embrace . . .

Fortunately, it's rarely too late to take positive steps toward owning who you are innately. Remember the poem, "When I Am Old I Shall Wear Purple?" *Now* is the time to metaphorically wear purple—or whatever color best suits your innate brain preferences.

And when you can do this with a family member or good friend who is on a similar journey of discovery and empowerment, so much the better.

Jon's Story

It was time for parent-teacher conferences. Sandwiched between his mother and father, Jon sat across the desk from his teacher. The boy looked at the floor as his father's words rushed out in bursts. "Miss Johnson, Jon is not getting A's in math and spelling. What are you going to do about it?"

Miss Johnson bit back both a smile and a retort. She wanted to say: *What am I going to do about it? Give me a break!* Instead, she asked the father, rather off handedly, "How did you like math and spelling in school?"

There was a decided pause, followed by another explosion of words. "I hated them both! Why do you think I'm insisting that Jon get A's? I don't want him to struggle in life like I've had to!" The father's already very square jaw jutted out even further.

Miss Johnson sighed. She'd experience this scenario far too often. *Why do so many parents place almost impossible expectations on their children? Especially when the parents had similar struggles!*

Since no definitive answer was forthcoming, she began to talk with Jon's parents about subjects where this teenager appeared to be gifted— music, art, computers.

"Balderdash!" Jon's father growled. "The computer market is flooded and he can't make a living at music and art."

Taking another tack, Miss Johnson asked the father what he did for a living. "I'm an accountant," the man bellowed. "And a darned good one." Miss Johnson remained silent.

Suddenly and without warning, the father's face turned red, and he lowered his head. "But I always wanted to be a chef," he said in low voice. Both Jon and his mother stared at the man in amazement. This was news to them—big news.

Seizing the opportunity, Miss Johnson planted some seeds in the father's mind about helping Jon find his own giftedness. Seeds about the difference between doing one's best versus feeling pressured to get A's in every subject. Seeds about Jon and his father enrolling at the local junior college for some evening classes in cooking and in art.

The best part was that Jon's father actually seemed open to the idea.

Imagine! Both father and son finding their own paths—together.

Iyanla Vanzant addressed this in *Acts of Faith:*

Many of us have said, 'I am tired of struggling!'
Well, guess what? . . . When you stop struggling,
things get better. Struggle goes against the flow.
It creates exhaustion in the mind and body.
When you are exhausted, you get sick. If you are
sick, you must make a decision and commitment
to do everything in your power to get better. The
power is in the commitment never to do what
makes you sick. The key is the decision
never to tire of doing what is best,
good, and right for you.

Live by Design

Your mind wants to grow and be stretched, to be discovered and energized. Even more importantly, it wants to be respected and honored. It wants you to collaborate with it, not by default, but by design.

Pablo Casals wrote: "And what do we teach our children in school? We teach them that two and two make four and that Paris is the capital of France. When will we also teach them what they are? We should say to each of them: 'Do you know what you are? You are a marvel. You are unique. In all the world there is no child exactly like you . . . You may become a Shakespeare, a Michelangelo, a Beethoven. You have the capacity for anything. Yes, you are a marvel."

Those powerful words could have been written about you—as an adult. You too are a marvel. Let your gifts shine through because there will never be another you. The new applications and personal experiences, in narrative or poetry or picture or dance, are for you to create.

You can't go back for a brand new start, but you can start from now—and make a brand new ending.

Empowered with this new information, your journey's just begun. As the song says, "We've only just *begun* to live."

> *Happiness is a journey, not a destination.*
> *So work like you don't need money.*
> *Love like you've never been hurt.*
> *And dance like no one is watching.*
> —Anonymous

It's time for you to make a difference. Go now. Create your own stories. Debunk the myths and invent new truths. Live your own innate preferences and create your own miracles.

Einstein once said, "Nothing happens until something moves." It's time to get moving. Get moving at the speed of life.

Yours!

After all, the life you save could be your own.

An Ancient Fable

Once upon a time, a long time ago, so the old fable goes, a native trapper found an eagle's egg.  Not knowing what else to do with it, the trapper slipped it into the nest of a prairie chicken and then continued on his way.

In due time the eggs hatched, the eaglet along with the rest of the clutch. The baby birds grew up together, believing they were siblings.

The eaglet, assuming it was a prairie chicken, did what good chicks did. They worked hard to learn the tricks of the trade and eventually became very competent in scratching for food on the wide prairie. So did the eaglet. Years passed.

One day, chancing to glance upward, the eagle noticed a magnificent bird far above in the cloudless sky. Hanging with graceful majesty on the powerful wind currents, the bird soared with scarcely a beat of its strong wings. At times, its shape momentarily blotted out light from the sun.

"What a spectacular bird," the eagle said to its prairie-chicken pal. "I wonder what it is."

"It's an eagle, of course," the prairie chicken replied. "The chief of birds!"

"Oh, to fly like that!" the eagle mused, its eyes filled with longing. "Just look at those aerobatics! Get a load of that wingspread!"

The eagle sat motionless for a very long time, gazing up at the chief of birds. The prairie chicken watched the eagle as it watched the bird in the sky. Finally the prairie chicken shook its head and chuckled. "Don't give it a second thought," he admonished.

"But . . ." the eagle began.

"You could never be like that bird. You can't fly. Prairie chickens don't fly—not like that!" The prairie chicken shook its head again.

So the eagle never gave it a second thought and went back to scratching for food on the wide prairie. Many years later the eagle died—still believing it was a chicken. Still believing that it, an eagle, was incapable of flying and soaring!

Translate that from the world of fowl to the world of human beings. Many a gifted individual has died either not knowing its giftedness or believing it was of little value. Thanks to dedicated researchers, brilliant observationists, untiring scientists, and modern inventors who have provided the world with brain-imaging modalities—we know better. Now that we know better, we can do better. Every one of us!

Point To Ponder

---

*It doesn't matter how well you walk the path—
if it's not your path.*

—I. Katherine Benziger PhD

Authors

Your brain is your greatest resource; use
it by design for success.
—A. R. Taylor

Arlene R. Taylor, PhD, one of the world's
leading speakers on brain function, is sometimes
referred to as the brain guru. She specializes in
simplifying this complex topic—thereby
assisting individuals to unleash their potential to
thrive. She has spoken to thousands of people at
conferences internationally. A sought-after
speaker, she presents practical brain function
information in entertaining, educational, and
empowering ways.

The brain-function information Taylor presents
is life-changing. Whether through keynote
addresses and seminars, or her internationally-
known books, CDs, and DVDs, success stories
pour in from many parts of the world.

Taylor is founder and president of Realizations
Inc, a non-profit corporation that promotes brain
function research and provides related
educational resources. She has earned doctorates
in Health & Human Services and in Clinical
Counseling. A member of the *National Speakers
Association*, Taylor is listed with the
Professional Speakers Bureau International.

According to world-renowned management consultant, W. Edwards Deming, "Learning is not compulsory . . . neither is survival."

Make a choice to continue *learning*. Examples of available resources follow:

SynapSez™ is a free quarterly online bulletin that provides current brain-function information, brain aerobic exercises, seminar schedules, and a variety of resources. To receive the Brain Bulletin, sign up at:

www.arlenetaylor.org

NOTE: Your e-mail address is never sold, rented, or shared, and you may unsubscribe at any time.

Books and DVDs - Taylor's books and selected DVDs are available on www.amazon.com.

These and other resources including CDs are also available on her web site.

Visit Taylor's web site at:

www.arlenetaylor.org

You may contact Dr. Taylor at:

thebrain@arlenetaylor.org

Authors, Cont'd

There is a close relationship between the mind and the body. In order to reach a high standard of intellectual attainment, the principles that control our physical being must be followed.
—*W. E. Brewer*

W. Eugene Brewer, EdD, senior partner in TriEd Associates, is an internationally-known educational development specialist, author, and guest lecturer. He has been principal at the elementary, middle, and high school levels, served as a superintendent in charge of forty-five schools and as a development specialist in curriculum and instruction. He was principal of a multi-cultural school with over fifty nationalities represented in the student body.

Using Jungian Psychology as a basis, Brewer researched the correlation of temperament types with brain quadrant preference. His work validated the use of temperament types and brain quadrant leads as models for adopting instructional strategies to address student diversity.

Brewer has presented at numerous conferences including the Learning/Brain Expo. He holds an EdD in Curriculum with emphasis on Learning Theory. He is co-author of *StudyWhiz: Self-Directed Learning Guide, Second Edition.*

StudyWhiz's goal is to change learners from passive, teacher-dependent students to active, confident, self-directed learners. It is an information management system that enhances memory and transfer.

Brewer is co-founder, educational consultant, and presenter for TriEd Associates. TriEd Associates brings focus to problems of strategic significance in the ever-changing world. The company provides a wide range of consulting services and products for educational organizations, educators, parents, community groups, and corporations with a unique blend of programs, staff development, and family training that focuses on the developmental needs and characteristics of today's youth.

Visit Brewer's web site at:

www.TriEdAssociates.com

You may contact Dr. Brewer at:

gbrewer@triedassociates.com

Sensory Preference Assessment

Identify Your Sensory Preference using the following assessment.

Instructions:

Read each of the following 63 statements. If the statement applies to you **at least 75% of the time,** place a one (1) on the line in front of the statement. If the statement applies to you **less than 75%** of the time, leave it blank.

    ____   1. I am very sensitive to odor/scents, taste, temperature, and texture.

    ____   2. I learn a lot about people from their voices (e. g., tone, volume, speed of speech, inflection)

    ____   3. I like to control the lighting in my environment (e g., dimmers, spotlights, up-lights, mood)

    ____   4. I can usually recognize objects quite easily by touch, even in the dark

    ____   5. Sounds catch my attention quickly

    ____   6. I purchase items primarily based on looks and visual appeal

_____ 7. I select clothes because they are comfortable to wear and feel good

_____ 8. When selecting a place to live, the available view is of major concern

_____ 9. I talk to myself frequently, silently, under my breath, or aloud

_____ 10. Room and comfort are very important considerations in buying a vehicle

_____ 11. I keep up with current events by listening to radio news more than by watching television

_____ 12. I tend to select clothes because they look good or sharp

_____ 13. I prefer frequent changes in body position and move often

_____ 14. I avoid wearing anything mismatched in color, pattern, or design

_____ 15. I would rather listen to a recorded book than read it

_____ 16. I like to keep my vehicle washed, waxed, and looking good

_____ 17. Others consider me chatty or may even say that I talk too much

_____ 18. I often use expressions such as "That fits" or "I've got a handle on it"

_____ 19. I prefer a map or diagram to receiving verbal or printed directions

_____ 20. I tend to "hear" the author's voice when reading written communication from people I know well

_____ 21. I enjoy engaging in physical exercise (e. g., walking, hiking, cycling, jogging, swimming)

____ 22. Strange noises or rattles in my vehicle or house annoy or worry me

____ 23. I like to work out and/or take jazzercise or yoga classes

____ 24. When eating, the presentation of the food, table, and environment is very important

____ 25. I talk to my pets as I would to close friends

____ 26. I learn a lot about people from their appearance

____ 27. I'd rather participate in sports than observe others playing

____ 28. I use rhyming words to help me remember names, labels, dates, or other facts

____ 29. I often see something before I hear, sense, or feel it

____ 30. I enjoy soaking in the tub or basking in the warm sunshine

____ 31. Jingles and acronyms help me to recall information

____ 32. I rarely bump into or stumble over objects I didn't see

____ 33. I like to receive and/or give back rubs and massages

____ 34. I enjoy touching and hugging my friends

____ 35. I prefer to see people when communicating with them

____ 36. I study for exams by verbalizing my notes and/or key points aloud

_____ 37. When shopping, I want the products to be clearly and attractively displayed

_____ 38. I repeat new words to myself to help fix them in memory

_____ 39. I readily learned the touch method for keyboard and/or data entry systems

_____ 40. I prefer pets that I can watch (e.g., fish in a tank, birds)

_____ 41. I have excellent physical coordination

_____ 42. I enjoy humming, whistling, or singing (alone or in a group)

_____ 43. I often say things like "That's crystal clear," or "I see what you mean"

_____ 44. I often use expressions such as, "Sounds right," "I hear you," or "Keep your ears open"

_____ 45. I learn a lot about people from their handshakes, hugs, or touch

_____ 46. A picture or diagram is worth 1000 words

_____ 47. I often tap my toes or want to move my body to music or a beat

_____ 48. I especially appreciate musical programs, concerts, or recordings

_____ 49. I like to hold babies or pets that I can touch, stroke, and cuddle

_____ 50. I prefer to watch TV, movies/DVDs rather than read the book or script

_____ 51. I like listening to talk shows or interview programs

____ 52. I especially enjoy making things with my hands (e.g., woodwork, carving, crocheting, knitting, sewing, finger painting, various crafts)

____ 53. I often enjoy verbal discussions in person or by phone/ham-radio

____ 54. I prefer books and magazines that contain colorful illustrations

____ 55. I prefer being outdoors rather than indoors whenever possible

____ 56. I really enjoy looking at photo albums

____ 57. I am usually considered an attentive listener

____ 58. Above all, my furniture must be comfortable

____ 59. I enjoy listening to recorded books, CDs, MP3, iPod, iPhone, et cetera

____ 60. It is important that my living/work spaces look visually attractive

____ 61. I prefer my home and vehicles to be climate-controlled for comfort

____ 62. Mirrors are important fixtures in my home

____ 63. I can't stand the sound of jingling keys or a dripping faucet

Identifying Your Sensory Preference

Transfer all your number ones (1) to the correct corresponding question numbers on the next page.

2 = ___	3 = ___	1 = ___
5 = ___	6 = ___	4 = ___
9 = ___	8 = ___	7 = ___
11 = ___	12 = ___	10 = ___
15 = ___	14 = ___	13 = ___
17 = ___	16 = ___	18 = ___
20 = ___	19 = ___	21 = ___
22 = ___	24 = ___	23 = ___
25 = ___	26 = ___	27 = ___
28 = ___	29 = ___	30 = ___
31 = ___	33 = ___	32 = ___
36 = ___	35 = ___	34 = ___
38 = ___	37 = ___	39 = ___
42 = ___	40 = ___	41 = ___
44 = ___	43 = ___	45 = ___
48 = ___	46 = ___	47 = ___
51 = ___	50 = ___	49 = ___
53 = ___	54 = ___	52 = ___
57 = ___	56 = ___	55 = ___
59 = ___	60 = ___	58 = ___
63 = ___	62 = ___	61 = ___

Add the points in each column.
Write the totals below.

Auditory	Visual	Kinesthetic
Column 1	Column 2	Column 3

The column with the highest score likely represents your overall sensory preference—the type of sensory stimuli that register most quickly and intensely in your brain.

If two scores are tied, one of those scores may indicate your sensory preference while the other may represent skills you developed in order to relate to someone significant in your life. If one of the tied scores is kinesthetic, consider the possibility that your innate preference may be kinesthetic, but for some reason you pulled back from it. Can you identify possible reasons that might have pushed you to do this?

If all scores are equal, this is not thought to be a naturally occurring pattern. Evaluate your sensory history to identify and uncover factors that may have influenced you to repress your sensory preference and build equal numbers of skills in the other two systems.

Sensory preference impacts on your energy levels, too. Your brain is believed to expend less energy to decode sensory stimuli that match your sensory preference. And as authors Loehr and Schwartz pointed out in their book *The Power of Full Engagement,* energy is the fundamental currency of high performance.

277

Point To Ponder

It's not what you think you are—but what you think, you are. The brain believes what you tell it most, and what you tell it about yourself it will create.

—Anonymous

Appendix B

Energy-Assessment Tool

Most people have heard comments such as, "I have so much fun at my job! I almost feel guilty taking a pay check!" Or, "You couldn't pay me enough to do that job. I get exhausted just thinking about it!" Differences in comments typically relate to brain energy and the relative amount expended on the specific activities involved at work.

To track energy expenditures, you first need to become aware of them. You can only manage effectively what you can identify and label. To some degree your energy expenditures are observable—to others often, and to yourself once you become aware of tracking them.

Even when you can't "observe" your energy expenditures directly, you can still observe your relative energy levels in relation to or in response to specific activities as compared against other activities.

Observation Example

Fold your hands, fingers interlocking, in your usual manner. Which thumb is on top? Right or left? Next, move your fingers one position so that you fold your hands with the opposite thumb on top. How does that feel?

Repeat this action. Pay close attention to how difficult or easy it is to accomplish, and how comfortable or uncomfortable your hands feel depending on how they are folded. You can do the same thing with crossing your arms. Each arm-folding style utilizes different amounts of energy.

The same thing happens inside your brain. Some activities utilize miniscule amounts of energy; others require exhausting amounts.

Activities Evaluation

Much in the same way as evaluating comfort of hand and arm folding, the following tool is designed to help you evaluate energy expenditures for activities related to your job or career.

Remember, your "job" is whatever you do to earn money or to contribute to a partnership that earns money. Our culture often defines this far too narrowly and incompletely. The individual who stays in the home and handles child care, household tasks, and a hundred other errands is "working" just as is the individual who is "working" at a location outside home base.

To really hit pay dirt in terms of energy evaluation, you need to analyze specific activities related to your work. Most jobs have a few key activities that, when taken together, comprise the majority of the job. After you have performed this evaluation a few times you will likely be able to do it with your mind's eye. To begin with, think of each activity in terms of three sections: pre, during, and post-activity.

Goal

The overall goal is to use the information from these tools to achieve an energy-efficient match between the majority (at least 51%) of your job-related activities and what your brain does energy efficiently (e.g., sometimes referred to as a brain lead or as your brain's innate energy advantage).

Outcome Benefit

The outcome benefit to you is the opportunity to manage your energy by design and, thereby, build a successful work life that can be sustained over time.

Taylor's Energy-Assessment Tool

Set #1: First, answer the following set of *Pre-Activity* questions to evaluate your energy levels as you think about a specific key activity that is required for your job.

For each question that you answer with a definite "yes," circle the numerical value in the right hand column.

Total the circled numbers in the value column when you have finished Set #1.

Set #1   Pre-Activity Questions   Value

1.	Do I dread the proposed activity because I sense it will drain my energy or because it has in the past?	1
2.	Do I try to delegate the activity, or get someone else to do it for me?	1
3.	Do I procrastinate working on the activity or reschedule it several times?	1
4.	Do I try to think up a plausible excuse in order to avoid the activity altogether?	1
5.	Do I feel neutral about the activity, neither negative nor positive?	2
6.	Do I expect the activity to be reasonable easy but don't want to spend much time on it?	2
7.	Do I look forward to the activity itself, or because it will be shared by a coworker I like to work with?	2
8.	Do I look forward to the activity with some anticipation as long as episodes are infrequent?	2
9.	Can I hardly wait to get going on the activity, and look forward to it with anticipation?	3
10.	If necessary, am I willing to rearrange my schedule (if possible) so I don't miss working on the activity?	3
11.	Do I look forward to spending time with the coworker as well as working on the activity?	3
12.	Am I willing to give up something desirable in its own right in order to spend time on this activity?	3
	Set #1 Total Score	

Set #2: Next, answer the following set of *During-Activity* questions.

For each question that you answer with a definite "yes," circle the numerical value in the right hand column.

Total the circled numbers in the value column when you have finished Set #2.

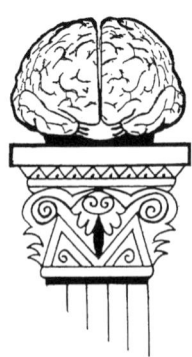

Set #2   During-Activity Questions   Value

1.	Do I spend the bare minimum of time on the activity and exit for almost any excuse (e.g., respond to my pager and gratefully define the interruption as an emergency)?	1
2.	Do I frequently sneak a look at my watch because time is dragging and I sense my energy is flagging?	1
3.	Do I make excuses, no matter how thin, in an effort to avoid doing the activity?	1
4.	Do I find myself swallowing retorts or biting back exclamations, or eating, drinking, or smoking more than I know is good for me out of boredom or irritation or fatigue?	1
5.	Do I enjoy some aspects of the activity but truly dislike others?	2
6.	Do I sense that the activity is essential and I'm glad to help even though it isn't particularly rewarding for me?	2
7.	Do I list the benefits of or reasons for the activity to help validate my need to keep doing it?	2
8.	Do I find the activity interesting and stimulating even though my coworkers are energy neutral?	2
9.	Do I feel excited or even energized within minutes of beginning the activity?	3
10.	Do I forget to look at my watch and can hardly believe how fast the time is flying by?	3
11.	Do I try to find ways to prolong working on the activity?	3
12.	Do I find myself thinking about the next time I can work on a similar activity, even before this one ends?	3
	Set #2 Total Score	

Set #3: Finally, answer the following set of ***Post-Activity*** questions.

For each question that you answer with a definite "yes," circle the numerical value in the right hand column.

Total the circled numbers in the value column when you have finished Set #3.

Set #3   Post-Activity Questions   Value

1.	Do I wipe the proverbial sweat from my brow with relief that the activity is finished?	1
2.	Do I go to bed early, or vegetate in front of the TV, or soak in the tub, because I'm so exhausted?	1
3.	Do I dread having to complete a similar activity in the future?	1
4.	Do I wonder how I am going to jump-start my flagging energy so I can finish the activity?	1
5.	Do I recall the activity with a sense of neutrality (e.g., it wasn't awful but it wasn't great either)?	2
6.	Do I know how to do the activity so well that I can think about something else (e.g., listen to books on tape or music) while I am working?	2
7.	Do I wish that others had been present to add some spice and variety, and then the activity wouldn't have seemed so boring?	2
8.	Do I applaud my choice to dig in and get the activity finished because I recognize the benefits received by myself or others?	2
9.	Do I recall the activity with pleasure, and with a sense of pride, accomplishment, or even nostalgia?	3
10.	Do I work on the activity even when it isn't absolutely required that I do so?	3
11.	Do I sense that I am more energetic overall than I was before beginning the activity?	3
12.	Do I anticipate with pleasure getting to work on a similar activity in the future?	3
	Set #3 Total Score	

Section Evaluation

Transfer your total score for each set of questions to the following boxes.

Set #1 Pre-Activity	Set #2 During-Activity	Set #3 Post-Activity
Total _____	Total _____	Total _____

Explanation of Section Scores

- **A score between 0 and 4** in any section indicates that the activity is likely an energy-drain to your brain. Meaning that your brain may expend 100 times the energy to complete the activity (as compared to those that are energy-efficient for your brain).

- **A score between 5 and 8** in any section indicates that the activity is likely energy-neutral for your brain. While it may not drain your energy it doesn't boost your energy levels, either.

- **A score between 9 and 12** in any section indicates that the activity is likely quite energy-efficient for your brain. Meaning that your brain expends a relatively small amount of energy when it is engaged in the activity.

Explanation of Overall Score

Add scores for all three columns.

Transfer your overall score to the following box.

Overall Score
Total _____

An overall score between 0 and 12

This suggests that the activity is energy-intensive for your brain. Ask yourself: Must you complete this activity yourself, or do you have any option for delegating it to someone for whom it would be at least energy neutral? If you need to continue doing the activity, try to *sandwich* it between other activities that are energy-neutral or energy-efficient for your brain.

If your entire job consists of energy-exhausting activities you may want to develop a game-plan that will enable you to move to another job where the majority of activities are a better match with your brain's innate energy advantage. If that isn't an option, you will need to get very centered about engaging in activities outside of work that match your brain's innate giftedness. After all, you want to live a lot of happy, successful years filled with life in those years!

An overall score between 13 and 24

This indicates that the activity is basically energy-neutral. While it doesn't drain your energy, it doesn't boost it, either.

Make conscious choices, whenever possible, about sandwiching the activity between other activities that are easier and more energy-efficient for your brain to complete.

An overall score between 25 and 36

This is a strong indication that the activity is *energy-efficient* for your brain. At times, working on the activity may actually provide your brain with the perception that it is gaining energy, because you may feel so energized and affirmed.

These are the types of activities that you want to engage in the majority of the time (e.g., at least 51% of the time).

Practical Application

If you recognize that there is a less-than-optimal match in your current job, ask yourself if you can tweak some of the activities to result in a better match with your brain's energy advantage? Or could you collaborate with others to achieve a better match for each person's brain?

If the answer to these questions is "yes," however tentative, try it. If that attempt works, try another little tweak. You may be surprised at the latitude you have in many jobs to implement this strategy.

Remember, your overall goal is to achieve a majority match between required activities and what your brain does energy-efficiently.

This doesn't mean you'll ever have a job where you don't have to *work.* That's what employers pay for, **work.** But a 51% match is doable in many jobs. And when a majority of required activities are energy-efficient for your brain, you may never want to retire. Just joking!

Seriously, your work life can feel like *forever* if there isn't a good match between who you are innately and the way in which your brain is being forced to function. A mismatch is not a good recipe for achieving extreme excellence!

On the other hand, if the answer to these questions is a resounding "NO!" you may want to start evaluating the possibility and probability of you obtaining a better match. If you are self-employed, you may have more options—but not necessarily. In fact, some employers are open to tweaking job descriptions in order to retain valued employees and increase revenues.

If your explorations of your present employment do not indicate the probability of obtaining a better brain-activity match, you may want to take steps toward making an eventual job change.

Bernie Segal has been quoted as saying, "Don't climb the ladder of success only to find it's leaning against the wrong wall".

For one thing, you need to be clear about your definition of *success*. Recognizing that your current job is a mismatch with what your brain does energy-efficiently may be the impetus you need to take another look at your passion. It might even prompt you to create an internal picture of your *ideal job* and then find a way to bring it into being. For some, that could mean following their bliss and finding a way to make money at it.

Conclusion

Many problems related to achieving a successful work life can be attributed to a less-than-desirable match between required activities and the energy expenditures they require. Will it take some time and energy to figure out which activities are a desirable match with your brain's innate giftedness and which are a less-than-desirable match because they result in huge expenditures of brain energy?

Absolutely.

Will the information you glean increase your risk for long-term success?

Definitely.

Knowledge is power. Identifying your brain's innate energy advantage can give you a leg-up on knowing which activities:

- You want to perform yourself

- Need to be traded out or hired out

- Can be accomplished quite effectively through collaboration with another brain or brains

Energy drain often gets in the way of your unique calling, what your brain is designed to do energy-efficiently. All things being equal, the more clearly you identify activities that match your brain's energy advantage, and the more consistently you obtain at least a 51% match between your life's activities and what your brain does energy-efficiently, the better.

And in the process, you risk not only improved health, but also enhanced relationships, higher levels of success long-term, and a thriving life that serves as a role-model to others. What's not to like?

Point To Ponder

Your profession is not what brings home your paycheck. Your profession is what you were put on earth to do with such passion and intensity that it becomes spiritual in calling.

—Vincent Van Gogh

Bibliography

Additional Brain Facts/References can be found on Taylor's web site:

http://www.arlenetaylor.org

Amen, Daniel G., MD. *Change Your Brain Change Your Life.* NY:Times Books, 1998.

Amen, Daniel G., MD. *Magnificent Mind at Any Age – Natural Ways to Unleash Your Brain's Maximum Potential.* NY:Harmony Books, 2008.

Benson, Herbert, MD., with Marg Stark. *Timeless Healing: the Power and Biology of Belief.* NY:Scribner, 1996.

Benson, Herbert, MD, with Miriam Z. Klipper. *The Relaxation Response.* NY:Avon Books, 1975.

Benson, Herbert, MD, with William Proctor. *Your Maximum Mind.* NY:Avon Books, 1987.

Benziger, I. Katherine, PhD. *Thriving In Mind: The Art of Using Your Whole Brain.* IL:KBA, 2006.

Bortz, Water M. II, MD. *We Live Too Short and Die Too Long.* NY:Select Books, 2007.

Bragdon, Allen D., and David Gamon, PhD. *Brains that Work a Little Bit Differently.* NY:Barnes and Noble Books, 2000.

Broadwell, Richard D., Editor. *Neuroscience, Memory and Language Decade of the Brain, Vol 1.* DC:Library of Congress, 1995.

Brooks, Robert, PhD, and Sam Goldstein, PhD. *The Power of Resilience.* NY:Contemporary Books, McGraw Hill, 2004.

Brynie, Faith Hickman. *101 Questions Your Brain Has Asked About Itself But Couldn't Answer, Until Now.* CT:Millbrook Press, 1998.

Buzan, Tony. *Make the Most of Your Mind.* KS:Fireside Books, 1984.

Carper, Jean. *Your Miracle Brain.* NY:HarperCollins Publishers, 2000.

Carter, Rita, Ed. *Exploring Consciousness.* CA:University of California Press, 1998.

Carter, Rita, Ed. *Mapping the Mind.* CA:University of California Press, 1998.

Childre, Doc Lew, Howard Martin, Donna Beech, and Institute of Heartmath. *The HeartMath Solution: The Institute of HeartMath's Revolutionary Program for Engaging the Power of the Heart's Intelligence.* NY:HarperOne, 2000.

Childre, Doc Lew and Deborah Rozman. *Overcoming Emotional Chaos.* CA:Jodere Group, 2002.

Cooper, Robert K., PhD., and Ayman Sawaf. *Executive EQ.* NY: Grosset/Putnam 1997.

Diamond, Marian, PhD, and Janet Hopson. *Magic Trees of the Mind.* NY:A Dutton Book, 1998.

Doidge, Norman, MD. *The Brain that Changes Itself.* NY:Penguin Books, 2007.

Einberger, Kirstin, and Sellick Janelle, MS. *Strengthen Your Mind.* MD:Health Professions Press, 2007.

Fisher, Helen, PhD. *Why Him? Why Her? Finding Real Love by Understanding Your Personality Type.* NY:Henry Holt & Company, 2009.

Goldberg, Elkhonon. *The Executive Brain.* NY:Oxford University Press, 2001.
Goleman, Daniel, PhD. *Emotional Intelligence.* NY:Bantam Books, 1995.

Goleman, Daniel, PhD. *Social Intelligence: The New Science of Human Relationships.* NY:Bantam Dell, 2007.

Goleman, Daniel, PhD. *Working with Emotional Intelligence* NY: Bantam Books, 1998.

Goleman, Daniel, PhD, with Richard Boyatzis, and Annie Mckee. *Primal Leadership.* Boston: Harvard Business School Press, 2002.

Gordon, Barry, MD PhD, and Lisa Berger. *Intelligent Memory.* NY:Penguin Group, 2003.

Greenwood-Robinson, Maggie, PhD. *20 / 20 Thinking.* NY:Avery, Putnam Special Markets, 2003.

Gurian, Michael, PhD. *From Boys to Men.* NY:Price Stern Sloan, Inc, 1999.

Gurian, Michael, PhD, and Patricia Henley, with Terry Trueman. *Boys and Girls Learn Differently!* CA:Jossey-Bass, 2001.

Gurian, Michael, PhD, and Barbara Annis. *Leadership and the Sexes.* CA:Jossey-Bass, 2008.

Jensen, Anabel L., PhD, et al. *Handle With Care: Emotional Intelligence Activity Book.* CA:Six Seconds, 1998.

Hafen, Brent Q., et al. *Mind/Body Health.* MA:Simon & Schuster, 1996.

Hammer, Dean H., and Peter Copeland. *Living with Our Genes: Why They Matter More Than You Think.* FL:Anchor, 1999.

Hart, Leslie A.. *Human Brain and Human Learning.* NY:Longman Inc., 1983.

Healy, Jane M., PhD. *Endangered Minds.* NY:Simon & Schuster, 1990.

Herrmann, Ned. *The Whole Brain Business Book.* NY:McGraw-Hill, 1996.

Hinton, S. E. *The Outsiders.* NY:Puffin Books, 1997.

Howard, Pierce J., PhD. *The Owner's Manual for the Brain. Everyday Applications from Mind-Brain Research.* GA:Bard Press, 1994, 2000.

Jensen, Anabel L., PhD, et al. *Handle With Care: Emotional Intelligence Activity Book.* NY:Six Seconds, 1998.

Koch, Richard. *The 80:20 Principle.* NY:Currency Doubleday, 1999.

LeDoux, Joseph. *Synaptic Self.* NY:Penguin Books, 2002.

Lazarus, Richard S., PhD. *Stress and Emotion: A New Synthesis.* NY:Springer, 2006.

Levine, Mel, MD. *A Mind at a Time.* NY:Simon & Schuster, 2002.

Loehr, Jim, and Tony Schwartz. *The Power of Full Engagement: Managing Energy, Not Time, Is the Key to High Performance and Personal Renewal.* NY:Free Press, 2004.

Lombard, Jay, Dr., and Dr. Christian Renna. *Balance Your Brain, Balance Your life.* NJ:John Wiley & Sons, Inc, 2004.

McGraw, Phillip C., PhD. *Self Matters, Creating Your Life From the Inside Out.* NY:Simon & Schuster Source, 2001.

Millan, Cesar. *Cesar's Way: the Natural, Everyday Guide to Understanding & Correcting Common Dog Problems.* NY:Harmony Books, 2006.

Milne, A. A., and Earnest H. Shepard. *The House at Pooh Corner.* NY:Puffin, 1992.

Morrison, Toni. *Jazz.* NY:Vintage, 2004.

Norden, Jeanette, PhD. *Understanding the Brain, Parts 1-3.* VA:The Teaching Company, 2007.

Ornstein, Robert, PhD. *The Roots of the Self.* NY:HarperCollins Publishing, 1995.

Ornstein, Robert, PhD, and Paul Ehrlich. *New World New Mind.* MA:Malor Books, 1989, 2000.

Pearsall, Paul, PhD. *The Heart's Code.* NY:Broadway Books, 1998.

Pert, Candace, B., PhD, and Nancy Marriott. *Everything You Need to Know to Feel Go(o)d.* CA:Hayhouse, 2007.

Pert, Candace, B., PhD. *To Feel Good: The Science and Spirit of Bliss* (Audiobook). CO:Sounds True Inc., 2007.

Pert, Candace, B., PhD. *Your Body is Your Subconscious Mind* (Audiobook). CO:Sounds True Inc., 2000.

Pert, Candace, B., PhD. *Molecules of Emotion.* NY:Scribner, 1997.

Ratey, John J. MD. *A User's Guide to the Brain.* NY:Vintage Books, 2002.

Ratey, John J. MD, and Eric Hagerman. *Spark: The Revolutionary New Science of Exercise and the Brain.* NY:Little, Brown and Company, 2008.

Restak, Richard, MD. *Mozart's Brain and the Fighter Pilot.* NY:Harmony Books, 2001.

Restak, Richard, MD. *Mysteries of the Mind.* Washington, DC: National Geographic, 2000.

Rosenthal, Norman, E., MD. *The Emotional Revolution.* NY:Citadel Press, 2003.

Rosenthal, Norman, E., MD. *Winter Blues. Revised Edition: Everything You Need to Know to Beat Seasonal Affective Disorder.* NY:Guilford Press, 2006.

Safire, William. *On Language.* NY:Avon Books, 1981.

Sapolsky, Robert M., PhD. *Why Zebras Don't Get Ulcers.* NY:W. H. Freeman and Company, 1994.

Schacter, Daniel L., PhD. *Searching For Memory: The Brain, The Mind, And The Past.* NY:Basic Books, 1997.

Schacter, Daniel L., PhD. *The Seven Sins of Memory: How the Mind Forgets and Remembers.* NY:Mariner Books, 2002.

Schwartz, Jeffrey M., MD, and Sharon Begley. *The Mind & the Brain.* NY:Regan Books, 2002.

Seaward, Brian Luke. *Achieving the Mind-Body-Spirit Connection: A Stress Management Workbook.* Boston:Jones and Bartlett Publishers Inc, 2004.

Siebert, Al, PhD, with foreword by Bernie Siegel, MD. *The Survivor Personality.* NY:Perigee Books, 1996.

Siegel, Daniel J. *The Developing Mind.* NY:The Guilford Press, 1999.

Singh, Dalip, PhD. *Emotional Intelligence at Work.* NY:Sage, 2000.

Sousa, David, EdD. *How the Brain Learns.* Third Edition. CA:Corwin Press, 2006.

Steinem, Gloria. *Revolution from Within: A Book of Self-Esteem.* NY:Little, Brown, and Company, 1993.

Stine, Jean Marie. *Double Your Brain Power.* NY:Prentice Hall, Inc, 1997.

Taylor, Arlene, R., PhD, and Sharlet M. Briggs, PhD. *Age-Proofing Your Brain.* CA:Success Resources International, 2009.

Taylor, Arlene, R., PhD, and Sharlet M. Briggs, PhD. *Age-Proofing Your Memory—the Ultimate Brain Builder.* CA:Success Resources International, 2008.

Townsend, John, PhD. *Who's Pushing Your Buttons.* TN:Integrity Publishers, 2004.

Whitehead, Alfred North. *Dialogues with Alfred North Whitehead.* Boston: Little Brown, 1954.

Williamson, Marianne. *A Return to Love:* Reflections on the Principles of 'A Course in Miracles.' NY:Harper, 1996.

Wilkins, Mary E.. *The Revolt of "Mother" and Other Stories.* NY:Dover Publications, 1998.

Wilson, Timothy D. *Strangers to Ourselves.* England: The Belknap Press of Harvard University Press, 2002.

Vanzant, Iyanla. *Acts of Faith.* KS:Fireside, 1993.

Zull, James, E., PhD. *The Art of Changing the Brain.* Virginia:Stylus Publishing, LLC, 2002.

Point To Ponder

The secret of geniuses' accomplishments does not lie in what they have, but in how they use their brains.

—Ann McGee-Cooper

Additional Books Authored or Co-authored by Taylor

Age-Proofing Your Brain (English and Korean)

Age-Proofing Your Memory (four versions)

Adventure Series:

- Adventures of the Littlest Dolphin
- Adventures of the Great White Owl
- Adventures of the Jungle Bully

Aimi Adventures Series:

- Aimi Adventures: The Startling Screech
- Aimi Adventures: The Birthday Dilemma
- Aimi Adventures: Jungle Gym Catastrophe
- Aimi Adventures: Secret Portrait Painter

Brain Benders (brain aerobic exercises for your neurons)